Easy ★ ★
MAGIC TRICKS

BOB LONGE

Sterling Publishing Co., Inc.
New York

Library of Congress Cataloging-in-Publication Data

Longe, Bob, 1928–
    Easy magic tricks/by Bob Longe ; illustrations by the author.
        p.   cm.
    Includes index.
    ISBN 0-8069-1264-2
    1. Tricks—Juvenile literature. 2. Conjuring—Juvenile
literature. [1. Magic tricks.] I. Title.
    GV1548.L57   1994
    793.8—dc20   94-11207
                                                                    CIP
                                                                    AC

10 9 8 7 6 5 4

First paperback edition published in 1995 by
Sterling Publishing Company, Inc.
387 Park Avenue South, New York, N.Y. 10016
© 1994 by Bob Longe
Distributed in Canada by Sterling Publishing
% Canadian Manda Group, One Atlantic Avenue, Suite 105
Toronto, Ontario, Canada M6K 3E7
Distributed in Great Britain and Europe by Cassell PLC
Wellington House, 125 Strand, London WC2R 0BB, England
Distributed in Australia by Capricorn Link (Australia) Pty Ltd.
P.O. Box 6651, Baulkham Hills, Business Centre, NSW 2153, Australia
Manufactured in the United States of America
All rights reserved

Sterling ISBN 0-8069-1264-2 Trade
                 0-8069-1265-0 Paper

Contents

INTRODUCTION

The magic tricks you'll find in this book not only fool, but they're also interesting, surprising, amusing—in a word, entertaining. None requires special dexterity, and only a few call for some degree of practice. The majority can be performed with everyday objects: cards, coins, string, rubber bands, safety pins, handkerchiefs, dice, and—always at hand, of course—your own fingers. Some tricks require props or gimmicks that can be constructed easily.

To help you achieve maximum impact, you'll be taught precisely how to perform each trick, including hints on patter.

Because I almost always use a comical approach when presenting tricks, many of these tricks stress humor.

TIPS

When You've Goofed

We're all familiar with the person who has an excuse for everything. *Nothing* is *ever* that person's fault. When a trick doesn't go right, you can recover and create amusement by pretending to be that person.

You might make such feeble excuses as:

"Of course that's the wrong card. I did that just to test you."

"So the string still has a knot in it. I did that on purpose. It's a joke. Ha-ha-ha-ha."

Or, the minute someone calls your attention to a mistake, instantly and very rapidly say, "I knew that." Then fill in with whatever preposterous excuse occurs to you.

The Joke's On You

Avoid making a fool of the spectator who assists you. Yes, the joke may be on him, but your manner should be kindly. If possible, share the role of victim with him. *Both* of you are astonished at the turn of events. Even better, make the joke turn on yourself as often as you can.

The Audience Is Your Friend

Please remember that you and the audience are sharing an experience. Together you're fooled, shocked, amazed, amused. You're just as surprised as everyone else. The audience (of whatever size) should not only like the tricks, but they should also like *you*.

ROUTINES

At the end of each chapter, I describe ways in which the tricks can be put together to make an entertaining routine. It makes little sense to do *one* card trick or *one* coin trick. Since the objects are right there, you might as well do several. There's no reason in the world why you shouldn't do a mix of card tricks, coin tricks, and tricks with other objects.

It's wise to plan to perform your tricks in a specific order. It helps you in two ways: (1) Since you include all the tricks when you practise the routine, you probably won't omit one in performance. (2) You'll never be at a loss; you'll always know which trick to do next.

Many good routines have a certain logical order to them. For example, the performer magically produces a coin and then does a trick with it. Most of the time, however, this "natural order" is itself an illusion. Most often the magician ties the tricks together with patter. Here's how you might do this. After performing a series of coin tricks, for instance, you might say, "Speaking of money, my grandfather used to put all his change into a handkerchief and then pin it closed." This gives you an excuse to take some safety pins *and* a handkerchief from your pocket. You can now perform tricks with either, or both. Any kind of comment to connect the tricks will do. In fact, audiences really enjoy it when the connection is rather silly. For the sake of humor, you might even make a point of the absurdity: "I know that sounds silly, but I couldn't think of any other way to work in a trick with these safety pins."

To develop a routine, there really are only four criteria: (1) The tricks should be good. (2) They should be tricks that *you* like. (3) There should be a variety of tricks, or a change of pace. (4) Your first trick should be an attention-getter, either something snappy or extremely interesting. Your last trick should be one of your very best.

STRING BANDS

String, cord, rope, or rubber bands are usually readily available. The tricks in this section can provide impromptu merriment.

String Out—1

Required is a length of string or cord about 4' (1.2 m) long. Tie the ends in a square knot. Stick your thumbs inside the loop and extend the string. Display the string at about neck level for all to see.

"Now here's a real riddle for you: Do I have a magic neck or a magic string? I'll let you decide."

Without removing your thumbs, swing the looped string over your head so that the string is behind your neck (Illus. 1). *For clarity, the string in all the string tricks is shown as thicker than it actually is.*

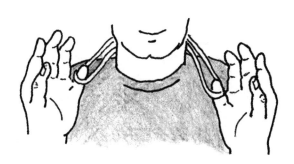

Illus. 1

"Now watch carefully."

Quickly bring your hands together and insert your left first finger into the loop just behind your right thumb. Pull to the right with your right thumb and pull to the left with your left first finger. Illus. 2 shows the beginning of this movement.

Illus. 2

Your left thumb naturally drops out of the loop, but only momentarily. Immediately, and without halting the motion, place your left thumb next to your left first finger and let the thumb take over the pulling motion to the left. Your left first finger will automatically be disengaged from the loop. Snap your thumbs against the inside of the loop as you extend the string forward. The position now is the same as at the beginning. Apparently, you've pulled the string through your neck!

The entire move is done in a fraction of a second. After you've practised it a half-dozen times, you'll have mastered it for life.

If you feel like it, you could perform the stunt just one more time.

Note

The trick may be done in other ways. You may, for example, pull the string through a belt loop. Most effective, perhaps, is to place the string around a spectator's arm and then, apparently, pull it right through his arm.

String Out—2

With that same looped string from the previous trick, you can perform another escape.

Hold the string between your two hands, fingers pointed towards yourself (Illus. 3). Bring the right side of the string *over* the left side, forming a small loop inside the larger loop

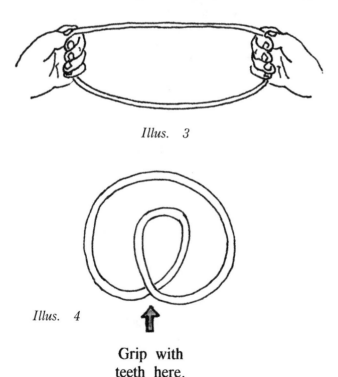

Illus. 3

Illus. 4

**Grip with
teeth here.**

(Illus. 4). Between your teeth, lightly hold the portion where the strings cross.

Stick your left thumb into the end of the larger loop, pulling it fairly tight, so that the smaller loop will be below it. Now, *from below*, stick your right first finger up through the smaller loop. Bring that finger over the right side of the larger loop, under the left side, and to your nose. The dark arrow in Illus. 5 shows the route of your first finger to your nose. Continue

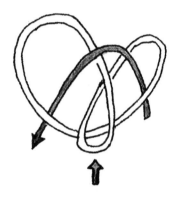

**Grip with
teeth here.**

Illus. 5

holding your right first finger to the tip of your nose as you pull the larger loop with your left thumb and release the string from your teeth. The string comes free, apparently passing right through your finger.

No Noose Is Good Noose

You can perform yet another unusual escape trick with that same looped string or cord.

"Here we have an enormous noose," you say, placing the loop over your head. At about the halfway point, cross the loop in front of your face and grip the crossing point between your teeth.

As clearly as you can under these adverse circumstances, say, "But this would be a much more effective hanging device if it were a *double* noose."

Cross the cord back again *the same way*, and place the rest of the loop back over your head. If you originally crossed the right-hand portion on top, it's vital that you recross it on top.

Mumble dramatically and indistinguishably about what a thrilling climax this wonderful trick will have. Grip the string on the right side with your right hand, open your mouth, and quickly pull the string off.

The Sliding Knot

A stage magician cuts a length of rope into two pieces and ties two of the ends together. A spectator holds the loose ends. The magician grasps the knot in the middle and *slides it right off the rope*, and the rope is completely restored!

I've always found this effect to be both amazing and amusing. Here's a version you can do with a pair of scissors and a 3' (1 m) length of string or cord.

Tie the ends of the cord together, forming a loop. Hold this loop between your hands, fingers pointed towards yourself. See Illus. 3 on page 11 for the proper position. Now, revolve your left hand, turning the string and forming a double loop. This is what spectators will assume you're doing. But in performance, you're much sneakier. When you form that double loop you give the string an extra half-turn with your left hand. Thus, when you stretch out the double loop, a portion of the string is interlocked, as shown in Illus. 6. Naturally, you don't want spectators to see this interlocked

portion. So, as you double the loop, quickly slide your right
hand along the doubled string and conceal the interlock.

Illus. 6

Move your left hand to within a few inches (cm) of your
right, so that you're offering a small length of string for Craig,
a helpful spectator, to cut with the scissors (Illus. 7). You

**Double-loop
concealed here.**

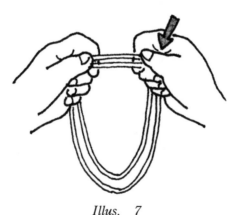

Illus.   7

very wisely handed Craig the scissors before you started
playing with the string. Invariably, your helper will cut at
about the middle of the portion offered.

Hold up the string in your right hand, demonstrating that
it's in two pieces. Making sure you keep the interlock concealed with your right fingers, carefully tie the ends of the

small piece into a square knot. Now you need no longer conceal anything.

Ask Craig to hold the two loose ends of the string. Make some mystical waves over the string, mumbling some magic words. Look a little disappointed. Try again. You're even more disappointed. "The magic doesn't seem to be working," you tell Craig. "But I'd like to give you a little something for helping out. I *know* you won't take money, so what can I give you? I've got it!" Slide the knot along the string, moving his hand to one side as you remove the knot from the string. Present him with the knot. Hold up the string by the ends. "Say! That *is* sort of magic."

And Slide Again

Using (about) a 3′ (1 m) piece of string or cord, you might try this trick, which is about as easy as magic ever gets.

Hold the string at one end and let it hang down. Ask Donna to point out the middle of the string. Take one end and tie it to the string at that point (Illus. 8). *Make sure you keep track of the portion leading to the knot, which is darkened in the illustration.* Ask Donna to cut the "middle of the string."

Illus. 8

Actually have her cut at the point indicated by the arrow in Illus. 8. Do so by holding the string between your hands and presenting only this portion to her.

Ask Donna to hold both ends of the string. You can now slide off the knot and present it to her, as you did in the previous trick. The following, however, might be a better conclusion. Hold the knot in your right fist. Bring your left hand over, apparently to take the knot. Actually, your left hand grips the point where the knot was, while your right hand slides the knot to your right. As you continue sliding the knot to the end of the string, say, "Could you pull the string a little tighter?" Move her hand aside with yours. She regrips the string, and you slide the knot off.

You can casually put your right hand in your pocket and leave the knot there as you massage the string with your left hand, restoring it. Or you can go your pocket for *magic dust*, leaving the knot there. The invisible *magic dust* is sprinkled over your left hand, bringing about the restoration of the string.

The Incredible Knot

G. W. Hunter invented this clever trick. You can use a 3' (1 m) length of string, cord, or rope.

You ask, "The question is, 'Can anyone tie a knot in a string without letting go of the ends?' The answer is no, unless you happen to be magical, a no-good sneak, or a lowdown rascal. And since I'm two out of three of those, I'll give it a try. Watch closely as I tie a knot without letting go of the ends."

Hold the string between your hands, as shown in Illus. 9. (For convenience the string is shown as shorter than it actually is.) Bring end B over your left wrist (Illus. 10) and around the back of your left hand to the position shown in

Illus. 11. Bring end B through the loop, as shown by the dark arrow in Illus. 11. Do *not* let go of end B.

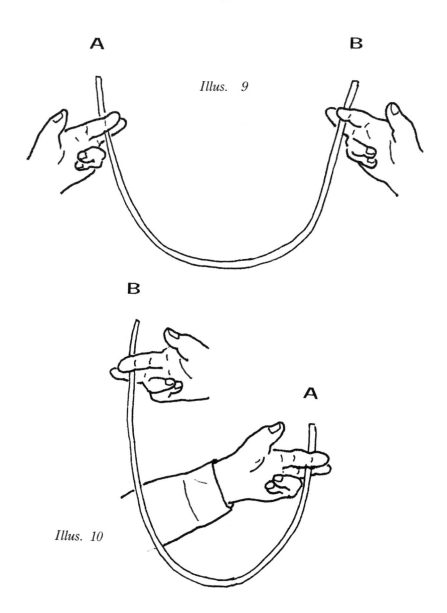

A   B

Illus. 9

B

A

Illus. 10

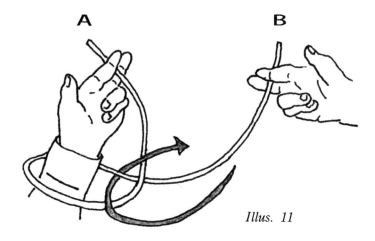

Illus. 11

Say, "I've done nothing underhanded—well, I have done something underhanded and (actually) overhanded—but nothing you haven't seen. The ends haven't left my fingers, yet the knot is already formed. But I do *not* use sleight of hand; I use *magic*. To prove it, I'm not going to do anything fast, or switch the ends, or do anything else sneaky." Address Mike, a spectator, "I want you to take one end in each hand and pull." When he does, a knot will form in the middle of the string.

Knot At All

Here's a simple, effective follow-up to the two preceding tricks.

Invite Martin and Wally to help out. Take the ends of your 3′ (1 m) string in your hands, about 5″ (13 cm) from the ends. Cross the right-hand section in front of the left (as you look at it) and grip the intersection between your left thumb and fingers. Pull End A through the loop (Illus. 12). Pull End

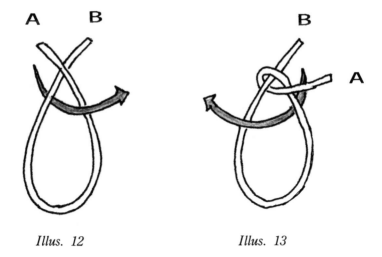

Illus. 12   *Illus. 13*

A to the right for several inches (cms) and then hand the end to Martin, asking him to hold that end for a moment.

Transfer the intersecting point (now a knot, but only briefly) to your right hand, so that you're now holding the point between your right thumb and fingers. Put End B through the loop, as indicated by the arrow shown in Illus. 13. Pull End B to the left for several inches, and hand that end to Wally.

Still covering the "knot" with your right hand, ask Martin and Wally to pull on the string. When the string is taut, say, "Whoa! You pulled too hard. The knot popped right off." Remove your right hand from the string and toss the invisible knot into the air. Invite them to examine the string—the knot's gone!

Or Knot To Be

Similar in *effect* to the preceding trick, this may well be the easiest method to cause a "knot" to disappear.

Take the ends of a 3′ (1 m) string and tie them together. Hold the loop in your hands, as shown in Illus. 3, on p. 11. Make sure that your right hand covers the knot.

Give the loop one complete twist (Illus. 14). This, in effect, divides the string into two loops. With your left hand,

Illus. 14

Grasp here.

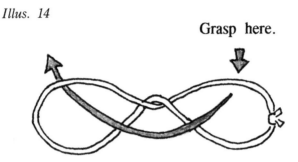

reach past the point where the string crosses, grasp one of the strands, and pull the strand through the loop on the left. The dark arrow in Illus. 14 shows this process. Pull the ends so that a knot forms in the middle. One of the strands (probably the top one) will slide through the knot. Say, "We'd better tighten the knot." Cover the knot with your left hand and pull on the appropriate strand with your right hand, sliding the knot to the left. When the knot is quite small, grip it tightly between your left thumb and left first finger. Jerk the strand with your right hand, pretending to tighten the knot. Actually, of course, the so-called knot can vanish by simply holding the string on either side of the knot and pulling on the other side. Go to the actual knot and, in similar fashion, tighten it. "Might as well tighten this one, too."

Go back to the false knot and grip it lightly between your left thumb and left first finger; your other fingers grip the string. "I need a lot more fibre in my diet. This could be a start." With your right hand, grasp the same strand it held before and pull the strand tight, popping the knot out of the string. At the same time, with your left hand, apparently pick off the knot and pop it into your mouth. As you chew and swallow, display the string, showing that the knot's gone.

Eye of the Needle

There's no particular relationship between the simplicity of a trick and the audience reaction. Here's a good example. The trick itself is very easy to perform, but the audience is usually astonished. What's more, because the result seems so impossible, *you'll* be delightfully surprised every time you perform it. To achieve this wonderful result, however, you must follow the instructions carefully.

You'll need a 3' (1 m) length of cord or string. Ask, "Has anyone here ever tried to thread a needle?" After the response, continue, "Well, I find it almost impossible. In fact, the *only* way I can do it is by resorting to magic. Let me show you what I mean."

Grasp the string about 8" (20 cm) from the bottom and wrap it around your thumb in a clockwise direction at least a half-dozen times. The string should be wrapped fairly loosely.

Illus. 15

Form a loop in the string, holding it between your left thumb and your left first finger (Illus. 15).

Display the loop, saying, "This is the eye of the needle." With your right fingers and thumb, grasp the 8″ (20 cm) length of string you let hang loose at the beginning. Hold it a few inches (cms) from the end. "This is the thread. You can see that the eye of this particular needle is enormous. Even so, I'll probably have difficulty threading it. But to make it even *more* difficult, I'll try to thread the needle—*without letting go of the thread*. Clearly, this calls for magic. So let me try my magic words:

> *Maybe my outstanding speed'll*
> *Help me push this through the needle.*

Now it's time for some great acting. With a quick forward movement, try to push the "thread" through the eye. Failure! Repeat the magic words and try again. Another failure! Again the magic words, and yet *another* failure. Say the magic words with great emphasis, and you'll finally succeed. Well, not actually. On your last attempt, brush the bottom of the loop with the bottom of your right hand, and then pull the string sharply upwards, letting a loop slip off your left thumb. It indeed looks as though you threaded the needle without letting go of the "thread."

Say, "It worked! So next time you want to thread a needle, try to remember the magic words."

As you'll discover, it takes some experimentation to get the moves exactly right, but the result is well worth the effort.

Candy Is Dandy

This is a trick in which you reveal the "secret" at the end. If you prefer, you could eliminate the last part and do the trick as straight magic.

All you need for this trick is a length of string, a handkerchief, and a roll of multicolored hole-in-the-middle candy.

In your right pocket you have a length of string and a candy, preferably light-colored. In your left pocket, you have a *bright-colored* candy at the bottom and a folded handkerchief well above it. On top of all this, you have a piece of candy which is the same color as the candy you have in your right pocket.

Reach into your right pocket and take out the candy and the string. Hold up the candy for all to see. Run the string through the hole, and then run one end of the string through the hole again so that the candy is held at the bottom of a

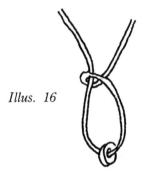

Illus. 16

loose loop (Illus. 16). This is done as misdirection; spectators might feel that there's something tricky about the way the candy is held on the string.

Get two spectators to hold the ends of the string. Reach into your left pocket. Grip the candy in your loosely curled fingers. Grasp a corner of the handkerchief between your first finger and thumb and pull the cloth from your pocket, snapping it open. Use both hands to lay the handkerchief over the string, concealing the candy that's hanging there.

Take the candy from your left hand into your right. Chat fairly loudly about the difficulty of the feat you're trying to perform; you're trying to cover any noise you might make as you break the candy that's hanging on the string. Make as clean a break as you can, because you don't want to deal with too many little pieces. Hold these pieces in your curled left fingers.

Hold the unbroken candy between your right fingertips and your right thumb. Drop your left hand down so that you can grasp an edge of the handkerchief between your first finger and your thumb. Whip the handkerchief off the string, and, with your right hand, hold up the candy for all to see.

Immediately, place the handkerchief into your left pocket. Shove the pieces of candy to the bottom of your left pocket. Grasp the multicolored candy and rest it on top of the handkerchief. Remove your hand from your pocket.

As you produce the liberated candy, some spectators may see through the trick. Don't let them analyze. Instantly say, "Don't say a word. I know exactly what you're thinking. Can he possibly do that again? Of course I can."

Quickly thread the candy onto the string, exactly as before. Have your assistants hold the ends of the string. Reach into your left pocket and take the bright-colored candy into your curled fingers. Grip the handkerchief between your thumb and your first finger and pull the handkerchief from your pocket. Be careful that you don't bring out any broken candy pieces along with the handkerchief. Proceed exactly as before. The broken pieces go into your left pocket, along with the handkerchief, and the liberated candy is held up for all to see.

There's one little problem: It's a different color! Stare at it for a moment in apparent shock. Say, "Oh-oh!" Pause briefly. Then say, "Real magic, ladies and gentlemen. Not only have I removed the candy from the string, but I've magically caused it to change color."

Join in with the general merriment. Sometimes a few of

the less astute in your audience will wonder what all the laughter is about.

A Bouncy Band

For this amusing stunt, you'll need two rubber bands.

Say, "Some people tie a piece of string around their finger to remind them of something. I use a rubber band. For example, I was supposed to buy one or two loaves of bread, so I put a rubber band around my first and second fingers." Place one rubber band over the first two fingers of your right hand, displaying it as shown in Illus. 17 (your view). Holding

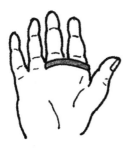

Illus. 17

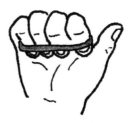

Illus. 18

the back of your right hand towards the onlookers, pull back the rubber band, using your left hand. Close the fingers of your right hand, so that when you release with your left hand, the rubber band will be outside all of your fingers (Illus. 18).

"Unfortunately, rubber bands aren't very reliable, so when I got to the store . . ." Straighten up your right-hand fingers. The rubber band will jump over, so that it will surround the other two fingers. ". . . the rubber band was on my third and fourth fingers. So I bought four loaves of bread."

Repeat the stunt, saying, "This kept happening to me every time I went to the store."

The feat you're about to perform is actually no more difficult than your first stunt, but it seems to be miraculous. "One day I decided to trap the rubber band so that it couldn't switch fingers on me."

Place the rubber band over the first two fingers of your right hand, as you did before. Pick up the other rubber band with your left hand and wrap it around the fingers of your right hand (Illus. 19).

Illus. 19

"But when I got to the store . . ." Follow the exact same procedure as before, and the rubber band will once again jump over so that it encircles the other two fingers. Shrug. "Again, four loaves of bread." Shake your head. "It didn't matter. I was supposed to buy *milk*, anyway."

That Band Really Jumps

It's always fun to involve a spectator in a funny bit of byplay. Ruth is supposed to have a great sense of humor; let's test it.

Place a rubber band on the first finger of your left hand, letting the band hang down (Illus. 20). Bring the band under your middle finger (Illus. 21), and then over the top of your middle finger. Hook the end of the band onto the tip of your

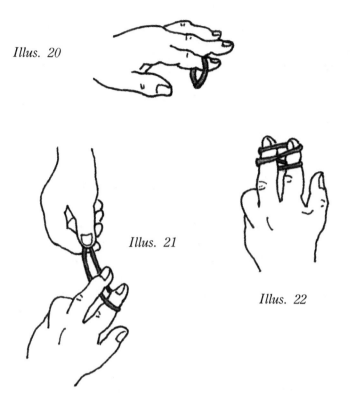

Illus. 20

Illus. 21

Illus. 22

first finger. Illus. 22 shows a simplified view of the final position. The rubber band should be at the very end of your fingers, attached between the first joint and the tip.

Hold your left hand upright, and ask Ruth to hold the tip of your first finger. When she does so, move back your middle finger, so that your finger is liberated from the rubber band. Instantly, the band will come loose from your first finger and end up around your middle finger.

Now it's time to display your performance skills. Stare at the rubber band with a puzzled look. Frown at Ruth. "I thought I asked you to hold my first finger. Let's try again."

Repeat the whole routine, admonishing Ruth," Now would you *please* hold on?" By the third time, she should really be squeezing the tip of your first finger. You might complain in mock seriousness, "Ow! That's tight enough."

You should probably quit after three or four tries, thanking Ruth for giving it a try. "After all, you did your best. It's probably not all your fault that it didn't work out."

Routine for String Bands

Pull a substantial length of string from your pocket or purse, and you're ready to perform an interesting five- to ten-minute routine. You might also carry a small pair of scissors with you.

You can actually perform the tricks in the order in which they appear in this chapter. For instance *String Out—1* (page 9), *String Out—2* (page 11), and *No Noose Is Good Noose* (page 12) are all escape tricks. You could begin with one or two of these.

The next two, *The Sliding Knot* (page 13), *And Slide Again* (page 15), are "cut-and-restore" tricks. Do at least one of these.

The theme of the next three tricks, *The Incredible Knot* (page 16), *Knot at All* (page 18), and *Or Knot to Be* (page 19), is magical knots. In the first of these, a knot is mysteriously formed, and, in the other two, a knot disappears. *The Incredible Knot* always goes over well, and I recommend that you do at least one of the others.

Eye of the Needle (page 21) is not only a good change of pace, but provides a startling climax to a series of string tricks. You may instead choose to close with *Candy is Dandy* (page 22), an excellent trick, which can either be done seriously, or, as described, for laughs. If you use it for laughs, it might be better as your second-to-last trick.

You may decide to perform the two rubber-band tricks some time in the midst of the string tricks, affording a touch of variety. Both *A Bouncy Band* (page 25) and *That Band Really Jumps* (page 26) are quite deceptive, and the latter evokes considerable laughter.

MENTAL MAGIC

Telepathy, ESP, precognition—little did you know that you possess all of these gifts! You can repeatedly demonstrate them in an entertaining fashion!

Telling Time

The first half of this is a regular trick; the second half is definitely a joke. Ask Carl to look at his watch or a clock (or to visualize a clock) and select two numbers that are opposite one another. He adds these together and tells you the result. You instantly tell him what the two numbers are. You even repeat the stunt a few times.

If you check your watch, you'll see that there are only six combinations:

$$1 + 7 = 8$$
$$2 + 8 = 10$$
$$3 + 9 = 12$$

$$4 + 10 = 14$$
$$5 + 11 = 16$$
$$6 + 12 = 18$$

If you know the total, you know the two numbers. It might take you a moment to solve, unless you thoroughly memorize the possibilities. I devised a simple method to enable you to give out the numbers immediately. At first, it might sound complicated, but a few trials will demonstrate that this method is quite easy. What's more, you'll never forget it.

When Carl tells you his total, divide that total by two, and then add three. This gives you one of the numbers. Subtract that number from the total given you, and you'll have the other number. Carl tells you that his total is 14, for instance. Divide it by two, giving you 7. Adding 3 gives you 10, one of the numbers. You announce this immediately. Then you subtract 10 from his total, 14, and you get 4, the other number.

Do this a few times. Now for some silliness. Speed is of the essence in this portion of the stunt. Move right along.

Point to Pete. "I'd like you to note two numbers that are directly opposite each other on a clock face. Got them? Now subtract the lower number from the higher. Okay? Concentrate on that. The resulting number is 6."

Quickly point to Patricia. "I'd like *you* to visualize two numbers on a clock face that are directly opposite each other. Subtract the lower number from the higher. Concentrate. The resulting number is six."

Point to another person, and start the routine again. I guarantee you that the group won't let you provide more than three examples of your telepathic ability.

Give 'Em the Slip

Here we have either magic at its finest, or the dumbest trick of all time. Some will think you're a *fabulous* magician.

You'll need eight little pieces of paper, so tear up a napkin or a sheet of paper.

Take a pen or a pencil, and, holding one of the pieces of paper in the palm of your hand (so that no one can see it), say, "Will someone please give me a first name?"

You write down the name of the piece of paper, fold the paper, and toss the paper on the table.

Take another piece of paper, ask for a name, write on the paper, fold it, and toss the paper on the table. Repeat the procedure for all eight pieces of paper. Mix up the slips.

"While I turn my head, I'd like you to pick out any one of the pieces." Someone does so. "Open it up and look at the name." Again, someone obliges. With head still averted, you say, "The name is Dennis." And, sure enough, you're right.

"Simple case of mental telepathy," you explain. Wait a few moments, gather up the other papers and discard them. If no one objects, you've performed a superb piece of magic.

But if someone troubles to open some of the other papers, he'll discover that the same name is written on each one, because you wrote the first name given on every slip!

In the first instance (if you discard the slips) you've performed a miracle; otherwise, you've presented a comical stunt.

Ergo

Dan Harlan told me about this trick; credit should go to John Bannon.

Spectators, while amused by this trick, will be at a loss to understand your logical process.

You'll need a deck of cards, and you'll have to force a card on a spectator. Three easy forces are available on pages 52–53. It doesn't matter which card you force, just so you know which one it is.

Let's suppose that you've forced the six of spades on Ron. Have him replace the card in the deck. Immediately hand him the deck and have him shuffle it. He continues to hold the deck while you proceed.

You say, "I've discovered that there's a strong relationship between a person's everyday activities and the sort of card he's likely to choose. For example, do you ever go to fast-food restaurants?"

Chances are that Ron will say yes. In all seriousness, you

say, "Uh-huh, just as I thought. It's pretty obvious that your chosen card is black. Which fast-food restaurant do you go to?"

Whatever he answers, you say, "I thought so. If I'm not mistaken, your card must be a spade. What kind of food do you usually order?"

Whatever his reply, you say, "Yes, an ordinary order. So your card isn't a face card; it has to be a spot card. Do you ever order french fries?"

He replies, and whether the answer is yes or no, say: "As I suspected, your card must be an even number. What do you order to drink?"

If he mentions a soda, ask, "Is that diet or regular?" Ron answers. "That's amazing. Your card is a six. The six of spades."

Clearly, there's no relationship whatever between his answers and your conclusions, but apparently *you* see some relationship.

The trick bears repeating with a different spectator. Only this time, base the questions on something else. Here are some possibilities: shopping habits, hobbies, music (favorite songs), television-show preferences, whatever.

Pursuing one theme, you might ask such questions as, "What color is your house? How many televisions do you own? Do you ever use a microwave oven? Do you have an automatic garage-door opener? What size is your bed?" In another category, you could ask, "What's your favorite fish? Do you like salad? What kind of bread do you prefer? What's your favorite dessert?"

The sillier the question, the better. Usually spectators will be smiling when you finish with your first revelation. As you work through the silly questions with your next assistant, many will be chuckling.

Mind Under Matter

George Sands discovered the principle; Martin Gardner invented the trick.

Grace seems to take ESP quite seriously. She's the perfect subject for this trick. Explain, "I'd like to check your ESP, Grace." Hand her a deck of cards. "Would you please remove the queen of spades and six other cards? As you know, the queen of spades is supposed to have mysterious powers, so I'd like to see how long it takes you to find her."

When she removes the seven cards, she'll probably have them face up on the table. Pick them up with the queen of spades at the face of the packet. Turn the packet over. In a series of casual overhand shuffles, move the queen to the top, then to the bottom, and then back to the top.

"Grace, I'd like you to choose a number from one to six." Suppose she names four. Hand her the packet. "Now I'd like you to move four cards from the top to the bottom, one at a time. Then turn over the next card." She does so. "No, it's not the queen of spades. Try again." Beginning with the face-up card, she again moves four from the top to the bottom of the packet and turns up the next card. Wrong again. In fact, she turns over six wrong cards in a row. At this point, you take the packet from her and fan through, showing that there's only one face-down card. Pull out the queen of spades and show it. "Wonderful, Grace! You have strong *negative* ESP." Place the queen of spades on the bottom and repeat the shuffling procedure, ending with the queen on top. Hand her the packet again.

"Try it again, Grace. Choose a different number." Once more the queen of spades is the last face-down card.

Perhaps one or two others would like to check out their ESP. They, too, will fail. The stunt can be repeated indefinitely, but three or four times should provide sufficient amusement.

You Can Count on Your Body

This very old trick originally involved several objects on a table and having a spectator think of one of them.

Get Hilda to volunteer, and say to her, "I'd like to point out different parts of my body." As you list each part, you touch it with one hand or the other. "Here we have my right hand, my left hand, my stomach, my throat, my mouth, my knee, my ear. Now please think of one of these as I go through them again. Right hand, left hand, stomach, throat, mouth, knee, ear." Again, touch each part as you name it.

"Now I'd like you to *mentally* spell the part you thought of as I go through the parts again. Start the spelling with the first part I touch, and each time I touch a part, think of the next letter in the spelling. When you've finished spelling the word, say, 'Stop!' "

The first two times, touch any of the listed parts. Then you touch parts in the reverse order of the list: ear, knee, mouth, throat, stomach, left hand, right hand. As you can see, the list progresses from a three-letter spelling to a nine-letter spelling. When Hilda says, "Stop!" you'll be touching the exact part she thought of.

Repeat the trick until everyone either catches on or grows tired of it.

Clearly, you may use other parts of the body if you choose, but you must start your list with a three-letter word, and then add one letter at a time to ensuing words.

Another option is to use the parts of someone *else's* body.

Blind Dates

With this stunt, you could impress people with your wizardry, or you could turn the trick into a farce. I, of course, prefer the latter.

Hand Adam a calendar and turn away. "I'd like you to pick out any calendar page and place your finger on the first day of that month. Now please add up that entire column, including the 1."

When Adam is done, say, "Please close up the calendar, but remember the number you ended up with."

Turn around and announce that the number is 75.

That's the trick, and a mighty fine example of omniscience it is. You may wish to continue.

Turn away and have someone else pick out a different calendar page. Give this person the same directions. Once more, after considerable concentration, announce that the number is 75.

You might even do it again. Sure enough, the number is 75.

The number is *always* 75!

One little problem. If your helper happens to pick February, the answer will be 46, unless it's a leap year. You can handle this in one of two ways: Prohibit the choice of February, indicating that it's your bad-luck month. Or, if you're told that 75 is incorrect, say "I meant 46. Why are you people trying to confuse me?"

How Oh-Old Are You?

Give Ethel a pencil and some paper. Turn your back and ask her to write down her age. She may lie, if she wishes.

Let's assume that she writes down 57 as her age. "Please add 70, which happens to be my lucky number. Got it? Now cross out the first digit. For example, if your number is 120, cross out the 1. Now add that digit to your new number. For instance, your number was 120 and you crossed out the 1. So your new number is 20. Add the 1 to that and you'll get 21."

Ethel has written 57. She adds 70, giving her 127. She

crosses out the first digit, 1. This leaves her with 27. She adds the 1 to 27, giving her 28.

You ask for the result, and then say, "Your age is 57. You really didn't have to overstate it that much. What is it really? 39? 40?" You'll never make anyone unhappy with this approach.

How did you know her age? You added 29 to the result she gave you. She said 28, you added 29, and came up with 57.

If asked to repeat the stunt, you can cause confusion by coming up with different lucky numbers. When 70 is your lucky number, add 29 to get the age. When you use 80, add 19. When you use 90, add 9.

One thing to keep in mind: The total of your lucky number and the person's age *must be* more than 100.

Gotcha!

You'll need a notepad measuring approximately 3″ × 5″ (7.5 × 13 cm). The sheets should be thick enough so that ink marks won't show through. Let's assume that you're going to predict the result of a hypothetical football game between the "Lions" and the "Bears." On the back of the top sheet, in the exact middle, print the word "Bears."

Now you're ready to make this proposal to the group: "Suppose the Lions and Bears are playing football. I'm going to write down here who I think will win." Holding the pad so that no one else can see, print the word "Lions" in the exact middle of the top sheet. Fold about a third of the sheet upwards (Illus. 23).

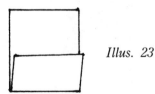

Illus. 23

Illus. 24

Tear off the sheet, and without letting anyone see the back, fold the top third *under* (Illus. 24). Toss the folded sheet onto the table. Later, depending on how you open the sheet, you can show either side. Practise the unfolding so that you can readily show whichever side you wish.

Ask the group to decide among themselves which team they think will win. When they finally decide, ask, "Are you sure? You can change your mind if you wish." When they're quite sure, unfold the sheet so that they can see that you've correctly predicted their choice. Crumple the sheet and put it into your pocket. Leaving your hand in your pocket, talk briefly about how even *you* don't understand the nature of your remarkable powers. Casually remove a crumpled paper from your pocket and toss it on the table as you continue to babble.

In nearly all instances, someone will take the crumpled paper and open it up. He'll read, "Gosh, you're nosy!" or some similar message.

That's right. Beforehand you placed a folded and crumpled sheet in your pocket with this message on it. You exchanged the papers in your pocket!

Routine for Mental Magic

Mind-reading tricks always go over well, so I recommend that you start off with *Telling Time* (page 30) *Give 'Em the Slip* (page 31). Although *Ergo* (page 32) is blatantly illogical, it's a puzzling follow-up to the previous two.

After demonstrating your own ESP, it can be fun testing it in others with *Mind Under Matter* (page 34). Continue the merriment with *You Can Count on Your Body* (page 35).

Next could come *Blind Dates* (page 35) and *How Oh-Old Are You?* (page 36) as unusual examples of your highly developed mental ability.

Close with *Gotcha!* (page 37), a very strong prediction trick.

HAPPY HANDS

In this chapter all the supplies you need are at your finger-tips.

Disjointed Digit

This trick works particularly well for children, but most adults are also amused by it. Apparently you remove the first finger of your right hand.

"I have some amazing feats for you. Actually, they're not feats, but hands. Just watch these magical fingers."

Wiggle your fingers, demonstrating their amazing flexibility. Position your left hand so that your fingers point down and the back of your hand is towards the spectators. Tuck your left thumb into your left palm. Bring your left hand in front of your right. Bend in the first finger of your right hand. Your left hand, of course, conceals this. Rest your left hand

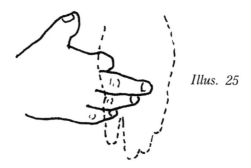

Illus. 25

on the back of your right hand, fingers still down (Illus. 25). The broken outline shows the position of your left hand.

"Watch carefully."

40

Twist your left hand upwards, raising the second, third, and fourth fingers. The first finger stays down, hiding the fact that your left thumb is bent inward. The illusion is that your left thumb is the outer joint of your right first finger (Illus. 26).

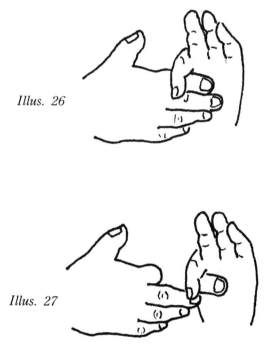

Illus. 26

Illus. 27

Move your thumb along the surface of your right second finger several times, demonstrating that the outer joint of your right first finger is separated from the rest of your finger (Illus. 27). Then, extend your left fingers again and straighten out your right first finger, grasping it in your left hand. Twist your right hand several times in a semicircle, "repairing" your finger. Hold up your right first finger and waggle it, showing that it's fully restored.

Incredible Shrinking Finger

You not only can remove one of your fingers, but you can also shrink one.

Hold up your left hand straight, back of your hand to the onlookers. Grip the little finger of your left hand with your right hand. The first finger and thumb of your right hand hold the top knuckle. The remaining fingers of your right hand are cupped outwards (Illus. 28).

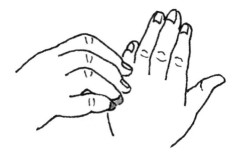

Illus. 28

Push downwards with your right thumb and first finger, holding the top of your finger straight. At the same time, however, bend the lower knuckle of your little finger outwards. You're concealing this bend with your second, third, and fourth right fingers.

Very slowly, push your little finger down, laboriously reducing its size. The illusion is quite realistic, since the tip of your finger remains pointing upward, and the finger slides down next to straight, extended fingers (Illus. 29).

Agonize as you pull your finger back up. Repeat the reduction. You might even try it a third time. Finally, pull your finger back up, grasp it with your right hand, and rub the

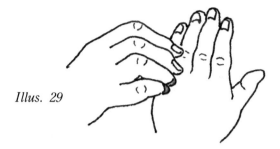

Illus. 29

finger vigorously. Then show your left hand, moving all the fingers to show that everything is as it should be.

Go Away

Some readers may remember this stunt from their childhood. It's amusing to those who've seen it before, and amazing to those who haven't.

You should be seated at a table. Tear off two bits of paper from a napkin, a tissue, or a paper towel. Moisten the bits of paper and stick one on the fingernail of each of your first fingers.

Place the tips of your first fingers on the edge of the table. Bouncing the two fingers rhythmically, you chant line one: "Two little birds sitting on a hill . . ."

Bounce the right finger as you say, "One named Jack, . . ."

Bounce the left finger as you say, "One named Jill."

"Go away, Jack." As you say this, swing your right hand up and past your head. During the swing up, fold in your first finger and extend your second finger. Instantly bring the hand down to the table, displaying the second finger.

Immediately say, "Go away, Jill." Perform the same switching action with your left hand. No one has time to observe what you actually did, because you proceed without hesitation to the next step.

Swing up your right hand again, and switch fingers again as you say, "Come back, Jack." Instantly do the same with your left hand, saying, "Come back, Jill."

Do not repeat the stunt.

The key is to perform the stunt *rapidly.* Once you start, the whole sequence should last no more than ten seconds. A few minutes' practice should give you complete mastery.

Here's the rhyme in one piece:

> *Two little birds sitting on a hill,*
> *One named Jack, one named Jill.*
> *Go away, Jack. Go away, Jill.*
> *Come back, Jack. Come back, Jill.*

Let's Go to the Hop!

Since the principle here is the same as that of *Go Away* (page 43), avoid doing both tricks for the same group at the same time.

Use any one of the following: a colored rubber band wound around your finger several times; an address label, moistened and attached to your finger; a scrap of thin paper (napkin, tissue), moistened and stuck on your finger; or a plastic bandage.

Illus. 30

Use the second finger of your right hand. Let's assume you've wound a colored plastic bandage around your second finger. Extend the first two fingers of your right hand. Make sure that the other fingers are well folded in, and that your thumb is out of sight (Illus. 30).

Hold out your left hand palm up; your right hand should be about 8″ (20 cm) above. Bring down your right hand to your left hand, displaying briefly the extended two fingers of your right hand. Leave your fingers there for only a fraction of a second—just long enough for onlookers to see them; then bring up your right hand to its original position. As you bring your right hand down again to display your fingers, fold in your first finger and extend your third finger (Illus. 31).

Illus. 31

"Watch it hop!" you say. Bring up your right hand again, and, as you bring it down, switch fingers once more. Repeat the switch several times *rapidly*. The illusion is that the label (or bandage) is hopping back and forth between your fingers.

Revolving Wrist

This brief, extraordinary stunt is a real reputation-maker. Apparently, you're either magical or double-jointed, for you can turn your hand completely around in a manner that's physically impossible.

To start, you must be wearing a suit jacket or sport coat, or the equivalent. For example, a sweater with long, loose sleeves will do.

Kneel down, press your hand against the floor, and turn your hand 360 degrees. It's quite impossible, and it looks ridiculous. When people see you do it, they'll either laugh or gasp.

The secret is quite simple, however, and you'll accomplish the feat easily on your first try. "Ladies and gentlemen," you might say, "I've been practising magic for some time. As a result, I've gained astonishing control over various parts of my body. Let me show you." Kneel down. Grasp your right sleeve with your left hand so that you can hold the sleeve in place while performing your maneuver. Turn your right hand palm-up and twist that hand counterclockwise as far as you can. Rest the *back of your right hand* on the floor (Illus. 32).

Illus. 32

You should be feeling some strain in your arm and wrist, but that sensation will be quite brief, for you'll begin the maneuver immediately. Very slowly rotate your arm clockwise, holding the sleeve so that it stays steady. Your hand, still pressed against the floor, also turns clockwise, of course. You strain a bit at the end to bring your hand to precisely the position it was in at the beginning. Illus. 33 shows your hand at various phases of the move.

Leave your hand in its final position for a few seconds, and then stand up, shaking your hand and arm.

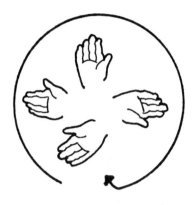

Illus. 33

Your audience asks, "How did you do that?" Don't tell them. If you do, you'll turn an astonishing feat into an insignificant little trick. *Don't repeat this trick*—at least not during that performance. Retrospectively, spectators assume that you started with your hand palm-down; don't destroy that illusion! The secret isn't well known, so keep it that way.

Sticky Knife—1

This *old* stunt is a perfect introduction to *Sticky Knife—2* (page 49) Ancient it might be, but this golden oldie will still provide oodles of fun.

Hold a table knife on your left palm with your left thumb
(Illus. 34). Grip your left wrist with your right hand. Turn

Illus. 34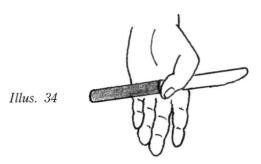

over your left hand, revolving your left land in your right
hand, which remains still. As you do this, turn your hand
downward, so that your left fingers point towards the floor.
At the same time, extend your right first finger so that it
holds the knife. Now stick out your left thumb, so that all can
see it (Illus. 35).

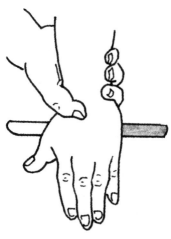

Illus. 35

Move your hands together, back and forth. The knife mysteriously clings to the palm of your left hand. Stop the movement and then precisely reverse the movements you performed when turning over your left hand. First, bring your left thumb onto the knife. Then revolve your left hand, palm up, as you return your right first finger to the side of your wrist.

Repeat the trick, if you wish. You might even consider teaching it to interested spectators. The next knife suspension, however, you *won't* teach; it's much too good a trick.

Sticky Knife—2

Hold up a table knife and say, "I'll now glue this to the palm of my hand." You attach the knife to your hands by interlocking your fingers, so that the second finger of your left hand is actually slid into the palm of your right hand, while your remaining fingers interlock alternately. As you interlock your fingers, slide the knife under your left second finger so that it's held secure against your right palm (Illus. 36). Don't

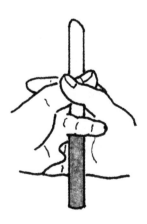

Illus. 36

perform this procedure in plain sight. If you're sitting at a table, take the knife under the table and attach it to your hands. If you're standing up, simply turn away for a moment while you perform the "dirty work."

Bring your hands and the knife into sight, the back of your hands towards the spectators, and the knife perpendicular to the floor. Hold your thumbs down so that onlookers will get the impression that your thumbs are holding the knife. Move your hands from side to side. "See? The knife is glued on." If no one comments about your thumbs, say, "You seem skeptical. The thumbs? Not at all." Raise your right thumb above your hand. "See? One thumb." Lower your right thumb and raise your left thumb. "And there's the other thumb."

Move your hands from side to side with your left thumb raised. If no one raises an objection, pretend to hear one. "Both thumbs? Oh, all right!"

Raise the other thumb. What? Your thumbs aren't holding the knife? But how . . .?

Wave your hands about, moving them backwards and forwards, side to side. Even tilt your hands, bringing them almost level, making sure no one can see your sneaky second finger, the one that's gripping the knife.

Abruptly separate your hands, taking the knife in one. Set down the knife and show both sides of your hands. No stickum, no rubber bands—just sheer magic!

This stunt may also be performed with a pencil, but I find it to be hard on my second finger.

Routine for Happy Hands

Since these tricks are so brief, several can be combined to fashion an interesting two-minute interlude. Begin with *Disjointed Digit* (page 40) and *Incredible Shrinking Finger* (page 42). Then choose either *Go Away* (page 43) or *Let's Go to the*

Hop (page 44). To cap the brief routine, do the astonishing *Revolving Wrist* (page 45).

Sticky Knife—1 (page 47) and *Sticky Knife—2* (page 49) can actually be tossed in anywhere, and the two should always be combined.

FORCES

Several of the following card tricks require forcing a particular card on a spectator. Here are three easy forces:

One-Cut Force. Learn the name of the top card. You could, for example, sneak a peek at the bottom card and shuffle it to the top. Have a spectator cut off a fairly large packet of cards from the top and turn them over on the deck. Immediately turn the deck over and spread the cards out on the table. You'll have a group of face-up cards followed by a group of face-down cars. Point to the first face-down card and ask the spectator to take the card and show it around. It is, of course, the force card. Turn the face-up cards face down and gather up the deck.

Double-Turnover Force. Again, you must know the top card of the deck. As you hold the cards, ask a spectator to cut off a small pile and place it face up on the deck. Then ask him to cut off a larger pile, turn it over, and place it on the deck. Fan through the face-up cards until you come to the first face-down card. Ask the spectator to remove the chosen card. It is, of course, the original top card of the deck.

Big-Deal Force. You must know the second card from the bottom. Fan through the face-up deck, saying, "Is the joker in here? We don't need the joker." Note the second card from the bottom. When you finish fanning through, say, "I guess not."

Now hold the deck in the dealing position in your left hand. Run your left thumb down the left edge, riffling the cards. Riffle all the way through the deck. Let's assume that a woman has agreed to assist you. Start riffling again, asking her to tell you when to stop. Make sure to riffle past the middle before she speaks up. Stop where she indicates and hand her all the cards below where you stopped.

"Now we'll do exactly the same thing." Have her deal her cards into a pile in front of her, one on top of the other. You deal the same way into a separate pile, matching her card for card. When she finishes, you'll have some cards remaining in your hand. Set these aside. Pick up the pile you dealt and have the woman pick up her pile. Place your top card in the middle. She does likewise. Place your bottom card in the middle. She does the same. "Now I'd like you to take your top card and set it on the table." She does so. This is the card which was originally second from the bottom. Now proceed with your trick.

CRAZY CARDS

All of these card tricks are designed both to amuse and to astound.

A Dizzy Spell

George F. Miller came up with an idea in which you *know* that the spectator's card is 37th from the top. I saw no quick way to reveal this fact, so I developed this trick.

You'll need a complete 52-card deck. Have Alan shuffle the cards. Take back the deck and quickly count off thirteen cards onto the table, saying, "We'll need 13 cards for this experiment, because, as you know, 13 is a mystic number." Quickly deal another 13 on top of these. "And we'll need another 13 to make things even more mystical."

Set the rest of the deck next to the first pile. You'll now have two piles (each with 26 cards) on the table.

"Please pick up either pile and shuffle it." After Alan does so, move the other pile to one side. Continue: "Seven, of course, is a very lucky number, so I want you to think of a number from one to seven. When I turn my back, remove that number of cards from your pile. You should hide those cards; put them in your pocket, sit on them, whatever." Turn away while this is done. When you turn back, take the remaining cards from Alan.

"Now I'll show you seven cards, and I'd like you to remember the card that lies at your number from the top." Hold the cards so that the faces are towards Alan. Take off the first card, and let Alan get a good look at it as you say, "One." Take off the second card and place it *in front of the first*, saying, "Two." Continue through the seventh card. You may close these cards up and casually place them on the bottom of the packet. Here, however, is a superior means of handling, which will require some practice: After showing the seven cards, close them up on top of the packet, holding a

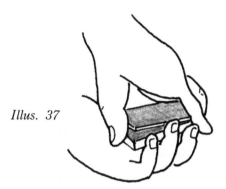

Illus. 37

break beneath them with the tip of your left little finger. Grip the deck from above in your right hand, transferring the break to your right thumb at the rear (Illus. 37). With your left hand, take off the bottom half of the packet and place it on top of the packet. Immediately take the remaining cards below the break (held by your right thumb) and place these on top. This sleight is known as a *double-cut*, and it effectively brings the seven cards to the bottom of the packet.

Continue, "Now, let me review what's happened so far. You thought of a number from one to seven and removed that number of cards. I showed you seven cards . . ." Fan out the top seven cards from the top of the deck, but keep them face down. ". . . and you noted the card at your number." As before, close up the seven cards and put them on the bottom. Instead, of course, you may once more do the double-cut just described.

The chosen card is now the 12th card from the top of the packet. Hand the cards to Alan. "I'd like you to spell out something, dealing off one card for each letter in the spelling.

Please spell out, 'This is my card.' " Coach him through it, as he spells out the sentence. Ask, "What's the name of your card?" Have him turn over the last card dealt. It's his card.

"Let's try it again with the other half of the deck." Set aside the cards that were just used. Ask Doris if she'll help out. Hand her the packet of 26 cards which haven't been used yet. Follow the same procedure as before. After she's noted the card at her number, place the seven cards on the bottom, or, as before, double-cut them to the bottom. Then say, "I don't think we'll need a review this time." The chosen card now lies 19th from the top of the packet. *Place the packet on top of the other pile on the table.* If Doris has chosen seven as her number, the chosen card will be at the bottom of the packet. When she spells out her sentence, the chosen card will be the last card in the packet. This isn't effective. Hand Doris the combined packets, asking her to spell out, "My card is lost forever."

After she does so, say, "Wrong, Doris! Your card isn't lost at all." Sure enough, the chosen card is the last card dealt in the spelling.

Note:

Use whatever sentences appeal to you to accomplish this trick. In the first instance, use any 12-letter sentence, such as, "I hope it works." In the second instance, use a 19-letter sentence.

Or Not

What could delight a spectator more than to see a magician fail again and again?

All the trickery necessary is to force a card on a spectator, or to learn the name of a chosen card after it's replaced. I prefer the former. Use one of the three easy forces described on pages 52 and 53.

Suppose you've forced the eight of hearts. You're now going to miss finding his card *seven* times. Hold the cards with the faces towards you. Fan through the deck and take out any heart except the (forced) chosen card. Smiling, hold the card in front of you, its back to the audience. "Your card is the seven of clubs," you announce. "No," you're told. *Immediately* say, "Or," dragging the word out, as you place the card face down on the table and frantically fan through the cards again. Remove another heart, holding it in front of you as before. "Your card is the nine of spades."

"No."

"Ooooor . . ." Place the card face down next to your first miss. The position in which you place your seven failures is shown in Illus. 38. Again you find a heart and announce the

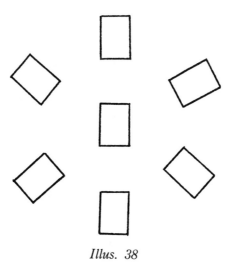

Illus. 38

name of some other card. As usual, you say, "Ooooor . . .," placing the card down next to the others.

In the same way, you miss on your next three guesses as you place three eights down on the table. Remember that, in our example, the eight of hearts was the chosen card. Finally, you remove the chosen card, name some other card, and place it face-down in the middle of your rejects.

Set the deck aside. "I give up," you say. "What was the suit of your card?" It was hearts, you're told. Turn up the outer three cards of the circle one by one. "What a coincidence! These are hearts! And what was the value?" You're told that the value was eight. Turn up the inner three cards of the circle one by one. "I can't believe it! These are eights. So your card was the eight of hearts." Indicate that the spectator should turn over the middle card. Wonderful!

A simple trick, to be sure. But properly acted, it can be most entertaining. In retrospect, many spectators will think you've performed a miracle. On more than one occasion, I've been requested to do that funny trick where I show different cards and then cause them to change to the suit and value of the one chosen.

One problem with this trick is that, with all the naming of the cards, it's easy to forget the name of the one chosen. Just repeat the name mentally to yourself as you go along.

Incidentally, your inspiration for the guesses can be a card adjacent to the one you're removing from the deck.

Say Cheez!

For some time, I've performed a marvelous sleight called *The Blow Change*: With a face-up card on top, raise the deck to your mouth, blow on it, and cause the card to change to another. The sleight is as easy to perform as it is deceptive. But I never had a *trick* to use with this sleight, so I developed the following, which always entertains. But first, here's the sleight itself.

Hold the deck in the regular dealing position in your left hand. Grasp the top card by its outer end and turn the card over, displaying it next to the deck and calling attention to its name. Meanwhile, secretly push off the present top card with your left thumb, and as you draw it back, secure a slight break beneath it with the tip of your left little finger (Illus. 39). Return the card in your right hand to the deck, keeping

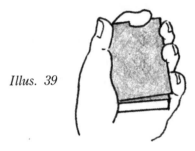

Illus. 39

it face up. The face-up card is precisely even with the card below it. Both are separated from the deck by the little-finger break.

You're about to perform *The Blow Change*. With your right hand, grip the two cards from above at the right side— thumb at the bottom edge, second finger at the top edge, and

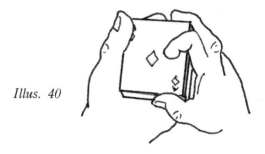

Illus. 40

first finger resting on the top surface (Illus. 40). Note that your left thumb is nearly removed from the deck.

Next, fairly rapidly raise the deck to within 1″ or 2″ (2.5 or 5 cm) of your mouth, retaining the grip of both hands. When the deck is almost perpendicular—about 6″ to 8″ (15 to 20 cm) from your mouth—lift the right edge of the two cards and, with a little aid from your left thumb, pivot the two cards over, so that their positions are reversed on top of the deck. As you reach a bit past the midpoint of the pivot, give a quick blow on the cards. Immediately begin lowering the cards to their starting position.

The pivot is complete, or nearly complete, and you've started lowering the cards. Note that your right thumb and second finger will be lightly gripping the *left* side of the deck. As you lower the cards, move your hand to the right, across the ends of the cards, and right off the deck. The illusion is that you simply moved your hand to the left and then the right as you straightened out the cards.

By the time your right hand is removed from the deck, the new card should be fully displayed. The entire maneuver takes about one second. Practise the move a bit and then try it in front of a mirror. You'll fool yourself!

Now for the trick! You must have on top of the deck the following cards, from the top down: jack, queen, king, joker. The suits are irrelevant. You may make this arrangement ahead of time. If you prefer, you can casually move these four cards to the top between tricks, making no attempt at secrecy. Then give the deck a riffle shuffle, keeping the four cards on top.

"There we are. I just finished putting the film in my camera, and I'm all ready to take some pictures." You'll receive some strange looks. "That's right. This is my camera." Hold up the deck. "It takes perfect pictures, and it develops them *instantly*. I'll show you."

Approach Naomi, holding the deck vertically in your left hand, as though you were going to take a picture with the face of the deck (Illus. 41). "May I take your picture?" She'll

probably agree. Tell Naomi, "Smile," or, "Say, 'Cheese.' "
Riffle the top end of the deck with your right fingers.

Illus. 41

"Perfect!" Take the deck in dealing position in your left
hand. Take the jack from the top of the deck, turn it face up,
and display it next to the deck, saying, "Here's Jack, the
instant developer." Meanwhile, you've obtained your little-
finger break under the queen. Place the jack face up on top
of the deck. "All we need now is a little air."

Perform *The Blow Change*, as described on page 58. Now
display the queen face up on top. "Ah, a perfect picture of the
beautiful lady." Hand her the card. "Here, look it over."

Immediately take a picture of Cal. Again you show Jack,
the instant developer, and perform *The Blow Change*. A king
is displayed on top. "A marvelous likeness." Hand Cal the
king.

For the last picture, choose Lowell, who's something of a
clown. With the aid of *The Blow Change*, Jack, the instant
developer, produces a joker. "Believe me, that's the real
you."

Look Ma, No Cards

Here's something different: a card trick without cards.

Ask Linda to assist you. Say, "I'd like you to think of a number from one to ten. This astonishing feat has nothing to do with a psychological choice, so I want you to change your mind. Got your number? Now double your number."

Wait a moment. "Add 14."

Wait again. "Divide by two."

Wait again. "Subtract your original number."

Wait once more. "That's the value of your card. Be sure to remember it. Now think of a suit. Got one? Put that together with your number and you have your chosen card. Please concentrate on your card."

Pretend to concentrate. You declare, "Your suit is hearts."

If the response is yes, you have a miracle. If not, say, "I was only kidding. Your suit is spades." Continue until you get the suit right.

When Linda finally says yes, say, "I can't believe you picked the seven of clubs (or whatever suit)."

Give it a chance to sink in; you have named the value of the chosen card. Then say, "Just another miracle."

Of course, you know the value. You gave the spectator the number 14, and the final number will be exactly half of 14. If you'd given the number 10, the final number would have been 5.

Happy Marriages

This entertaining routine with kings and queens combines three different tricks.

Remove the kings and queens from the deck, tossing them

one by one into a face-up pile. As you do so, say, "Some marriages are made in heaven. And some are made *elsewhere*! But in the wonderful world of cards, all marriages are very happy."

Pick up the pile of kings and queens and fan it out, faces towards you. Arrange the cards so that the kings and queens of matching suits are together. A typical order, from the top down, might be: KS, QS, KD QD, KC QC, KH QH. Display the cards in a fan. "See. All the couples just love being together." Place the packet face down on the table and ask that the packet be given a few complete cuts.

Pick up the packet and put it behind your back. Push off the top card with your left thumb and take the card between your right thumb and first finger. Push off the next card with your left thumb and take the card between your right first finger and second finger. Take the third card between your right thumb and first finger, *above* the first card. Take the fourth card between your right first finger and second finger, *above* the second card. Continue alternating until the pile is exhausted. Now you're holding two separate piles in your right hand. Take one of these piles into your left hand. Bring both hands forward and show that the kings are together in one group, and the queens in another.

As you arrange the cards behind your back, say, "Quite often, the boys would get together to watch a sports event on television, and the ladies would get together for an evening of cards." When you bring the two piles forward, say, "Here we see that the men are all enjoying a baseball game, while the ladies are playing a friendly game of bridge."

Take one pile on top of the other. At this point, the kings and queens should be in the same suit order. Place the pile on the table and have the pile cut a few times.

Take the pile behind your back. Without changing the order, separate the top four and place them between your left thumb and first finger. The lower four go between your left first finger and left second finger. With your right hand, remove a card from the top of each group and bring the pair forward. Turn the pair face up, showing that the king and queen match. Do the same for the next three pairs. As you do this, comment, "In a perfect marriage, the couples always get back together . . . as you can see."

Now casually place the kings on the table in a face-down row. First, place down the king of clubs. To the right of it, place the king of hearts. To the right of that, the king of spades. And at the far right, the king of diamonds. (Remember this order through the mnemonic CHaSeD.) Hand a spectator the face-up queens. Say, "Since playing cards have been around for hundreds of years, card marriages are very strong. And the king and queen in each marriage have a strong affinity for one another. Let's demonstrate. Place a queen face up on top of each king, in any order you wish."

After the spectator does this, there are several possibilities. If fate is kind, the spectator will match the pairs perfectly, in which case you simply show each pair. This turn of events is unlikely, however. *You* know that the kings lie, from left to right, clubs, hearts, spades, diamonds. Here are the other possible combinations: (1) four nonmatches; (2) one match, three nonmatches; (3) two matches; two nonmatches.

Suppose you have four nonmatches. Pick up the pair on the left, which has the king of clubs beneath, and place it on top of the pair which has the queen of clubs on top, thus placing the king of clubs face-to-face with the queen of clubs. Let's suppose this is the third pair in the row. You know that the bottom card is a spade, so place the entire packet on the pair that has the queen of spades on top. Then, place the entire packet on top of the remaining pair. Pick up the packet and fan the cards out a bit so that you can cut a face-down card to the top. All the pairs are now matched face-to-face. Deal off the top card face up and, on top of it, deal its mate.

Do the same with the other pairs, dealing them in a row. "Four perfect marriages," you declare.

Suppose you have one match and three nonmatches. Take the queen of the matching pair and slide it under its mate, saying, "I wonder if these two match." Leave this pair alone for a moment. Deal with the three nonmatches exactly as above, placing the kings face-to-face with their mates. As above, cut the three pairs so that a face-down card is at the top. Drop the packet onto the matching pair. All the pairs now match face-to-face, so you can finish as you did above.

The only tricky combination is two matches and two non-matches. Place one matching pair on top of the other and pick up the two pairs. Let's assume that the top card is the club queen and the third card down is the heart queen. Move the club queen to the bottom, saying, "Here we have the queen of clubs." Move the second card to the bottom, revealing the heart queen. Say, "And here we have the queen of hearts. Let's see if they match up." Take the queen of hearts into your right hand and, with the card's left edge, flip over the king of hearts. Take off the two face-up cards together, with the king lowermost, and set them on the table. Do exactly the same with the other pair. "That worked well; let's try the other pairs."

Place one nonmatching pair on top of the other. In our example, the queens will be the spade queen and the dia-mond queen. Place the spade queen on the bottom, saying, "Here we have the queen of spades." Place the next card on the bottom, revealing the queen of diamonds. As you do this, say, "And here we have the queen of diamonds." Before you complete the statement, *also place the queen of diamonds on the bottom*. "Now let's see if these match up."

Deal the top card (the diamond king in our example) face up onto the table. Deal its mate on top of it. Do the same with the other pair. All looks fair, with a face-up queen on top of each matching face-up king.

Practise the matching of mates for a half-hour or so, and you'll have mastered this trick.

What's in a Name?

Dan Harlan showed me this trick and credited Tom Craven for the idea; my only contribution is the conclusion.

Hand the deck to a spectator and ask him to shuffle the cards. If you don't know the spectator's name, ask him. Let's say he replies, "Wilbur Smith."

"Perfect!" you say. "This is a Wilbur Smith card trick." Pause for a moment. "Now please spell that out, dealing one card into a pile for each letter in the sentence."

Wilbur will probably be puzzled. Explain that he is to spell out the sentence, "This is a Wilbur Smith card trick," dealing out one card for each letter.

When he's done, ask him to set the deck aside and pick up the pile he has dealt. Turn away and give these instructions: "Please think of a number from one to ten. Very quietly count that number of cards back onto the deck from your pile." Pause. "Next, look at the card that lies at that number from the top of your pile. For example, if you counted three cards back on the top of the deck, you would look at the card that lies third from the top of your pile. That is your chosen card. Let everyone see it, but make sure it stays at that same number from the top."

When he's finished, turn back and ask, "What's your lucky number? Don't give me the same number you counted back onto the deck." Suppose he says, "Seven." Have him move seven cards from the top to the bottom of the pile, one card at a time.

"My lucky number is eight," you declare. Ask him to move eight cards from the top to the bottom in the same way.

"What kind of a trick is this?" you ask. If no one has the

right answer, you provide it: "This is a Wilbur Smith card trick. So, Wilbur, I'd like you to spell out your name, moving one card from the top to the bottom of your pile for each letter in the spelling. Use your complete name—Wilbur Smith."

When he's done, the chosen card will be on top. Ask him to name his chosen card, and then to turn over the top card on his pile.

All you have to do is to make sure that the total of his lucky number and your lucky number is 15. For instance, if his lucky number is 4, you must choose 11. In the above example, Wilbur chose 7, so you chose 8.

Note

For a repeat, have Mabel Jones assist you. Have her spell out "This is a Mabel Jones card trick," dealing off one card for each letter in the spelling. You turn away. As with Wilbur, she deals some cards back onto the deck and then looks at the card that lies at that number from the top of her pile.

Turn back and ask what kind of a trick this is. The correct answer is, "This is a Mabel Jones card trick."

"So, Mabel," you say, "I'd like you to spell out something else. This time, however, I want you to move one card from the top to the bottom of your pile for each letter in the spelling. Please spell, 'Mabel Jones will be astounded.' "

Help her along as she spells out the sentence. Ask her to name her card, and then have her turn over the top card of her pile. That card will be the one she selected.

One-Two-Three

Martin Gardner discovered the basic principle of this trick. Bob Hummer and Max Abrams added to and improved it.

The effect of this trick is that the magician names the one card of three a spectator thought of. This version is fairly amusing and can be repeated indefinitely.

Remove from the deck the ace, two, and three of diamonds, saying to Arlene, "I'd like to check your psychic abilities."

Lay the cards out so that they look like this from your view:

A   2   3

Think of them as *1, 2, 3*. "While my back is turned" you say, "I'd like you to think of one of these cards, then turn it face down. Then I want you to reverse the positions of the other two cards and turn them face down. For example, if you were to think of the three, you'd turn it face down." Now do exactly that and turn the three face down. "And you'd reverse the positions of the other two and place them face down." Pick up the ace and two and reverse their positions, as you turn them face down.

Turn the cards face up and return them to their 1—2—3 order. While your back is turned, Arlene follows your directions. Face her. Gather up the cards by placing the card on your right on top of the middle card, and then both on top of the card on your left. "Now we'll mix them up so that we'll both be equally confused."

Hold the three cards in the dealing position in your left hand. With your right hand, transfer cards quite rapidly from the top to the bottom of your pile. Each time, move either one or two cards. The total transferred must be 10. For instance, place the top card on the bottom. Then fan off two cards and place them in the same order on the bottom. Transfer two more cards in the same way. Move one card to the bottom. Once more, move a single card to the bottom. Now transfer two, and finally transfer one.

As you move the cards, mentally count them. In the example, you'd count, "One, three, five, six, seven, nine, ten."

Each time you repeat the trick, vary the manner in which you select either one or two cards, making sure that the total is always 10.

Now rapidly deal out the three cards face down like this: The top card goes in the middle, the second card goes on the right, and the third card goes on the left.

Say to Arlene, "We're about to check your psychic powers. I want you to pick out one card. But when you turn over that one card, don't let me know whether it's your card. You see, we want to also check *my* psychic powers. Now please turn one over."

She does so, and you instantly tell her whether she's right. How? Visualize the cards on the table like this:

$$3 \quad 2 \quad 1$$

Note that this is the reverse of the original layout. Suppose that Arlene turns over the card at 1. If it's the ace, she's picked out her original selection. Say, "That's right. That *is* your card." Congratulate her on her astonishing powers and perform the stunt again.

Suppose she turns over the card at position 2, and the card is the two. She's found her card. The same is true if she turns over the card at position 3, and it's the three.

But what if Arlene misses? You instantly say, "No, no, you were supposed to turn over the two (or whatever)," and begin to repeat the trick by laying out the cards face up in their original order.

How did you know her card? Simple. Suppose she turns over the card at position 1, and it's a three. Her card is the missing number: the two. If she turns over the two at position 1, her card is the missing number: the three.

Another example: Arlene turns over the card at position 2, and it's the three. The missing number is one, so the selected card is the ace.

Repeat the trick at least three times. This is one of those rare tricks in which repetition increases the mystery.

The amusement arises from the casual way you "throw away" the revelation of the chosen card. "No, no, you were supposed to turn over the two," you say, apparently unaware that you're doing something magical. As you repeat the trick, it seems to your audience that you *always* know the selected card instantly.

Note

When transferring cards from the top to the bottom, you may move 10, 13, 16, 19, etc. A total of ten seems sufficiently confusing to most spectators.

3–D

Stewart James inspired this trick.

"I call this my 3–D experiment," you say, fanning through a face-up deck of cards. "I'm trying to find a card here that jumps out at me, just as things seem to jump out at you in a 3–D movie. If my psychic abilities are operating, I should know—in advance—which card will be chosen." Find the three of diamonds and cut the deck so that the three becomes the second card from the bottom. "I'm starting to get the picture."

Ask Beverly to help you. Perform the *Big-Deal Force* (page 52). As she duplicates your movements with her packet, keep repeating *3–D*, saying such things as, "I hope my 3–D experiment works."

At the end of the force, tell Beverly, "I'd like you to take your top card and set it on the table." She does so, placing the three of diamond face down on the table. "Please take a peek at it all, and we'll find out if the 3–D experiment worked." She peeks at the card. You ask, "Did the 3–D experiment work?" Beverly will probably be puzzled. Have her turn the card face up. "It worked!" you declare. Pause to let this sink in.

"3–D," you say, "And the card is the three . . . of diamonds. Three stands for three, and D stands for Diamonds. 3–D! It worked."

Now ask Charles to help you. Explain, "I want to *prove* that I can actually foresee the future." (Downplay the word "foresee" at this point.) Fan through the face-up cards, studying them. Cut the four of clubs to the top of the deck. Then fan through once more, apparently still trying to fix on a card. Shake your head and close up the cards.

Now perform the *Double-Turnover Force* (page 52). At the conclusion of the force, ask Charles to remove his chosen card and place it face down on the table.

"The question is," you say, "did I foresee the future, or did I *not* foresee the future?" Pause. "Charles, please take a peek at the card." He does so. "Well, did I foresee it?"

Maybe he'll have caught on by this time. Regardless, have him turn the card face up. "There it is—4–C. Four stands for four, and C stands for clubs. 4–C!"

Super Stack

If the explanation of this trick seems a little complicated, don't be put off. After you've run through the trick a few times, you'll find that it's quite simple.

A stack is required, but presents no problems. Since it's obvious that the deck is stacked, don't pretend that it isn't. I do the stack in front of the spectators, chatting with them about a gambling story I want to tell them. "For this to work," I tell them, "I need all the right cards." You can't get any more honest than that. "The story is about a con man," you might add, "so naturally he uses a stacked deck."

While discussing the treat the spectators have in store, I fan through the deck, face towards myself, and push up the kings, the tens, and two inconspicuous spot cards. I remove these from the deck. I place them on top, and then sort the top ten cards so that, from top to bottom, this is their order: 10 (black), 10 (red), 10 (black), king, 10 (red), king, king, any spot card, king, any spot card.

First, the basic trick; then I'll take you through it with suggested patter.

You'll deal two hands, one to a spectator and one to yourself. Do this eight times. The first three times, you deal only three cards to each hand. Tell the spectators that you can deal three tens whenever you feel like it.

Now deal two three-card hands, one to your assistant and one to yourself. Instead of dealing the last card on top of your other two, you use the last card to scoop up the other two; thus, it becomes the bottom card of the three. All three are immediately placed on top of the deck.

Turn over the spectator's three cards. From the face, they'll be a black ten, another black ten, and a red ten. Take the black ten at the face and use it to scoop up the other two tens. All three are turned face down and placed on top of the pack. Once more you have on top, in order, a black ten, a red ten, a black ten, a king, a red ten, and a king.

Obviously, you're ready for a repeat. You can deal three tens in this fashion any number of times. Three times seems about right. Yes, the red ten changes each time, but people don't seem to notice.

From now on, you're going to deal five-card hands. On the first three of these hands, deal to your assistant full houses, each consisting of three tens and two kings.

For the first full house, deal two five-card hands, one to yourself and one to a spectator. Use your last card to scoop up the other four in your hand, just as you did with the tens, and all five are put on top of the deck. Turn over the spectator's hand, showing the full house. *Don't scoop.* Turn the full house face down and place it on top of the deck.

It's clear sailing the rest of the way. *You'll do no more scooping.* Simply deal five-card hands to the spectator and yourself, always returning your hand to the top first—*without scooping.*

Deal the second full house and return the cards to the top. Do the same with the third full house. In the gambling story, the character played by the spectator says, "That's no big deal. It's automatic." Have him deal the next hand, doing exactly what you did. Make sure he places his cards on top of the deck when he finishes the deal. Display the hand he dealt you. No full house. Take the deck back and place your cards on top.

Now for the big climax. Deal out two more hands. Leave your cards on the table instead of placing them on the deck. He turns over his hand. He has four tens. But you have him whipped, for you have four kings.

Here are the deals:

(1) The spectator gets three tens. Deal two three-card hands. With your last card, scoop the other two and place all on top. Turn over the spectator's hand. Take the card at the face and scoop up the other two. Place all face down on top.

(2) Same as above, and (3) Same as above.

(4) The spectator gets a full house. Deal two five-card hands, scooping up your four with the last card and placing all five on top. The spectator's hand is shown and placed on top.

(5) The spectator gets a full house. Deal two five-card

hands. Without scooping, place your hand on top. Show the spectator's hand and place it on top.

(6) Same as above.

(7) The spectator deals once as in (5) and (6), but you don't get a full house. His hand goes on top first. After showing your hand, it also goes on top.

(8) You deal two five-card hands, leaving both on the table. The spectator gets four tens; you get four kings.

Now for the patter and a more complete explanation. If you follow my suggestion for patter, you'll need a good-natured, relatively outgoing assistant, either a man or a woman. Continue your patter like this:

"This story is actually about a con man *and* a wiseguy. Please hold the applause until the end. I'd like to get a volunteer to play Willie the Wiseguy or perhaps Wanda the Wisegal. Don't hold back; this is definitely a speaking part."

While doing the recruiting and chatting, set up the deck. Let's assume that the volunteer is a woman.

"Okay, Wanda. Carl the Con Man—that's me—was at a party one evening and said, 'I'll bet I can deal three tens to myself any time I want to.' Wanda who'd come to the party alone, said . . ."

Nod to your assistant, indicating that she's to deliver a line. She'll probably say something like, "I'll bet you can't." If she says something totally different, however, like, "Who cares?", give her a line, like, "I'll bet you, you can't." When she delivers her line, express approval. In fact, do so after every one of her lines.

"So Carl said, 'You're on, lady.' And he dealt the hand."

Deal the first three-card hand. Place your cards on the deck, as described. Show the three tens in the assistant's hand and place the cards on the deck.

"Wanda had a hot temper and was very stubborn. So she said . . ."

Your assistant delivers a line. If necessary, have your helper change it to, "I'll bet you can't do it again."

Repeat the deal of the three tens, and then once more with similar patter.

"Carl the Con Man said, 'See? I can deal three of a kind any time I want to in three-card poker.' " 'But,' said Wanda . . ."

Point to your assistant. Her line should be: "But poker isn't played with three cards. You should deal five cards."

" 'That's easy,' said Carl. 'With five-card hands, I can deal full houses.' Wanda bets a certain amount of money that he can't."

Deal two five-card hands, scooping up yours with the last card dealt and putting your hand on top. Remember, this is the last time you scoop. For the remainder of the hands, you simply place your cards on top without scooping. Show the full house and put the cards on top.

Deal two more full houses, repeating the betting procedure. After dealing the third full house, say, "Wanda, who was really getting irritated, said . . ."

Your assistant will probably come up with an amusing line. After she does, have her do this line: "That's no big deal. It's automatic. I'll bet I could do it."

Give her the cards, telling her to deal exactly as you did, putting her hand on top after dealing the last card. Show that you don't have a full house. Take the cards from your assistant and place your hand on top.

"So Carl pocketed the ten bucks and said, 'See? Only I can deal a full house. I'll show you again free of charge.' "

Deal two five-card hands and leave them both on the table.

"Wanda looked at her hand and said . . ."

Have your assistant say, "I don't have a full house, but I'll bet you any amount I have you beat."

"Now don't forget, Carl is a con man. He said, 'No, I don't

tell you what: If I lose, I'll give you back your money; if you want any more of your money. But I don't have a car, so I'll lose, you give me a ride home.' She agreed by saying . . ."

Have your assistant deliver a line.

Indicate that she's to turn over her cards. She has four tens.

"Carl said, 'Four tens! Good hand. But if I recall correctly, this still beats four tens.' "

Face your hand one card at a time, showing the four kings.

"Carl said, 'You lose. You have to drive me home.' "

Have your assistant say, "Okay. Where do you live?"

"And Carl said . . ." Name some city several hundred miles away. There should be a chuckle or two, after which you add, "And the moral of the story is . . ."

Have your assistant provide a moral; chances are it will be silly and funny.

Note

If you prefer, speed things up by eliminating the assistant; simply tell the story, playing both parts yourself.

The Great Nancini

Phil Goldstein invented this trick based on a principle discovered by Jack Vosburgh.

Ostensibly, a spectator performs the trick. Take the first name of the spectator and put -*ini* at the end. Gloria, for example, becomes The Great Glorini; Fred is The Great Fredini.

The trick is based on the fact that three of the four aces are "pointer" cards. On each of the three aces, the pip "points" either up or down; therefore, you can tell when one has been turned end for end. If you remove the aces from a deck, you'll see what I mean. Turn the ace of spades so that its stem is down. Turn the ace of clubs so that its stem is down. Turn the ace of hearts so that its point is down. In other words, turn all three so that they're in a normal, right-side-up position. Now mix the four aces face down and turn one end for end. Mix them again. Look at the faces and you can instantly tell which has been turned; it will be the one *not* pointing in the same direction as the other two. If all point the same way, the ace of diamonds is the one that was turned.

Now for the trick. Ask Nancy and Bruce to assist you. As you chat with them, remove the four aces from the deck. Place them in a face-up pile, making sure that the three pointers are pointed in the same direction. This is easily done. As you take an ace from the deck, either deal it down directly, or casually turn it end for end as you place it down.

Ask Nancy if she'll be the magician. When she accepts, announce, "Ladies and gentlemen, The Great Nancini has consented to perform one of her world-renowned miracles for us. I'll get things started." Hand Bruce the aces. "Bruce, please mix them up, as best you can. Maybe give them some overhand shuffles." When he finishes, say, "Now pick out one card and give me the rest." When he hands you the cards, immediately hand them to Nancy. This subtly turns the three aces end for end.

"Show the card around, Bruce. Now The Great Nancini will have you replace your card among the others." After Bruce replaces his card, have Nancy hand the packet to him. "Mix the cards again, Bruce, just as you did before."

Take the cards from Bruce and look over the faces. Note which one was selected. Remember, it is the one which is *not* pointed in the same direction as the other two; or, if they are all pointed properly, it is the ace of diamonds. "Perfect!" you declare. "These cards are thoroughly mixed."

Hand the cards to Nancy. "Now The Great Nancini will reveal which one of the aces you chose. But, Bruce, don't tell her if she got it right or not. She may want to think it over." Turn to Nancy. "If The Great Nancini is ready, pick out the right card and hold it up for us."

If she picks out the chosen card, say, "The Great Nancini has done it again! That's right, isn't it, Bruce? A nice hand for the most wonderful magician of all . . . The Great Nancini!"

If she has the wrong card, immediately say, "No, that's wrong. I'm afraid that The Great Nancini has missed. Try again, oh great one."

If she gets it, instantly go into your first spiel. Otherwise, say, "Oh-oh, she missed again. Yes, Nancini has missed two in a row. This in itself is a miracle. Try again."

If she misses a third time, say, "No, no, wrong again. Try once more."

Since only one card is left, she'll probably get it right. Immediately praise The Great Nancini to the skies.

Needless to say, the trick provides the opportunity for all sorts of additional humorous comments.

Tell Me True

Paul Curry invented this trick; it should be done as you sit at a table. Sitting opposite should be the person you choose to assist you.

Besides a deck of cards, you will need a 3″ × 5″ (7.5 × 13 cm) file card. Fold in both ends of the card about an inch (2.5 cm), so that the card can be stood up. On the side that folds in, print this message: LIAR, LIAR, PANTS ON FIRE! Have the card in your pocket. Later, you'll stand it in front of you so that the message faces you and is upside down (Illus. 42).

Illus. 42

After shuffling the deck, sneak a peek at the bottom card. You might, for instance, even up the cards by casually tapping the side of the deck on the table, glimpsing the bottom card. Ask Joy to assist you. Set the deck on the table and ask her to cut off a pile of cards. She picks up the card she cut to, looks at it, and shows it around. Push the original top portion of the deck forward. Tap the top card, saying, "Place your card here, please." After she does so, say, "Now put the others on top."

Joy may now give the deck several complete cuts. It doesn't matter, because you now know the card above the chosen card.

Take out the file card and show the back. "I have a magical file card here which is going to assist me with this experiment." Stand the file card on the table in front of you, as shown in Illus. 42.

"Joy, I'd like you to pick up the deck. Take off the top card, name it, and place it *face down* on the table, but don't let me see the card. Continue through the deck, and when you come to your chosen card, I want you to lie. In other words, don't name your chosen card, name some other card. Remember, don't let me see the face of any card."

When Joy names the card you peeked at on the bottom, part your lips slightly. As soon as she names the next card, surreptitiously blow lightly on the file card. It falls forward; its message declares that Joy has lied. To enhance the effect, jerk slightly when the card falls, indicating that you, too, are surprised.

"The magic file card is never wrong," you declare. "That last one must have been your card."

A Five Spot

Wally Wilson called my attention to this trick.

Take the ten of diamonds from an old deck and tear it in half so that there are only five spots on each half of the card. Discard one half and keep the other half face-outward in one of your pockets.

In performance, fan rapidly through the deck and cut the five of diamonds to the top. You must force this card on a spectator—Gail, for example. Use either the *One-Cut Force* or the *Double-Turnover Force* (page 52).

After Gail returns the card, shuffle the deck, saying, "I'm going to cause your card to magically move from the deck to my pocket." Riffle the ends of the cards. "That should do it."

Pull the half-card (ten of diamonds) partially from your pocket so that all can see the value and some of the pips. "Here it is!" Gail denies this. "But your card is a diamond, isn't it?" Gail agrees. "And how many spots did it have?" Gail says, "Five spots." Pull the card all the way out of your pocket, saying, "If I'm not mistaken, *this* has five spots!"

The Hole Card

If you're a fast talker, you may get away with this trick.

Peek at the bottom card of the deck and shuffle it to the top. Deal the top card onto the table, saying, "That's my hole card. This is a funny game. Nobody else gets one."

Suppose the card you peeked at was the nine of clubs; here's how to proceed.

Turn to Kimberley, saying, "Red or black?" She says, "Red." You say, "That leaves me black."

It's Kate's turn. "Clubs or spades, Kate?" She says, "Clubs." You say, "Good choice. We've got clubs."

"Donna, spot card or face card?" She says, "Face card."
You say, "So I've got the spot cards."
Walt is eager to participate, so you say to him "High or
low?" He says, "Low." You say, "So I've got high. Six,
seven, eight, nine, ten." Turn to Herb. "Odd or even, Herb?" He says, "Odd." You
say, "So we've got a club, a spot card, odd and high. Seven
or nine."
Back to Kimberley. "Seven or nine, Kim?" She chooses
seven. You say, "So I've got nine, and I've got clubs. The
nine of clubs."
Turn over the card on the table, revealing that the group
has correctly named your hole card.
Clearly, you must practise this, proceeding briskly. Even
those who have an idea of what you're up to will be im-
pressed, or at least amused.
A repetition will evoke smiles and chuckles as nearly everyone catches on.

Can't See It

No skill whatever is required for this trick; the spectators will
have fun, and everyone will think you've performed a real
miracle. But you'll need a confederate—Eddie, for example.
Before you start, place a card into your pocket, let's say the
six of diamonds. Eddie must remember the name of this
card.
To perform, remove an invisible deck from your pocket.
Shuffle the cards as though they were real. "Here we have a
deck which many people have trouble seeing. Address Harriet: "I think you can see these, Harriet. How about helping
me out?" Hand her the invisible deck and instruct her to give
it a good shuffle. "I think Eddie can see the cards, too.
Harriet, please fan out the cards with the faces towards
Eddie. As she does this, Eddie, I'd like you to think of any
card you see."

After the business is done (usually to the considerable amusement of the group), take the invisible cards back, shuffle them, and put then into the pocket where you have the six of diamonds.

Ask Eddie to name his card. He, of course, says, "The six of diamonds." You reach into your pocket, fumble for a moment, and then bring out the six of diamonds, its back to the group. Snap the card and turn it around. Yet another miracle!

A Real Prince

You must have the four jacks on top of the deck, so it might be best to make this your first trick. Remove the deck from its case and set the deck face down on the table. Ask a male spectator to help out. Ray might be a good choice. Thank him for volunteering in these words: "I appreciate this. You're a real prince."

Ask Ray to cut off a packet of cards and to set the packet on the table. Pick up the remaining cards and place them crosswise on the packet. "The important thing is that you have complete freedom of choice," you explain. Actually, you're blathering to help everyone forget the relative position of the crossed packets on the table. Take off the upper packet and hand it to Ray, saying, "I'd like you to shuffle these thoroughly. Then pick out a card, look at it, show it around, and then place it on top of the pile on the table." After he's put his card on top of the pile on the table, say to Ray, "Now shuffle your cards again and then place them on top of the pile on the table." After he does so, have the deck given at least two complete cuts.

Pick up the deck and fan through the cards, faces toward yourself. "My job is to figure out which one of these is your card." Fan past the four jacks and the card above them. Cut the deck at this point, bringing the chosen card to the top and, below it, the four jacks. "While we're waiting, let's try a face-up and face-down experiment."

Deal five cards in a face-down row in front of you. Above the five, deal five face-up cards. This is the layout from your view:

face-up cards		×	×	×	×	×
face-down-cards		chosen card	J	J	J	J

Hand the rest of the deck to Ray, saying, "I'd like you to shuffle the deck and then deal a face-down card on top of each one of the cards on the table. You can deal in any order you wish."

When he finishes, take the deck from him and set it aside.

"Now we'll mix the cards a bit." Pick up the pair containing the chosen card and hold it face down in your left hand. Note and remember the face-up card of the pair on the far upper right; this is your key card. Pick up the pair, containing the key card, saying, "Each pair can be turned over or left as it is. Then each pair can be placed either on the top or the bottom." As you mention that the pair can be turned over, turn it over. But *be sure to turn it back*, so that your key card is still face up. Place this pair *below* the pair in your left hand.

Pick up one of the pairs containing a jack. "The same for this pair." Make a gesture as though to turn the pair over, but don't reveal the jack on the bottom. Place this pair on top of the two pairs in your left hand.

"Now you'll choose the order in which we add the pairs to the pile."

Have Ray tell you how he wants you to deal with the other pairs; do as he directs. Or, if he seems cooperative, have him do it himself. Emphasize the fact that he has three choices: (1) He can choose any pair. (2) The pair can be turned over or left as it is. (3) The pair can be placed either on the top or bottom of the packet. It doesn't matter whether a jack is revealed here and there as the pairs are collected.

When all the pairs have been gathered, even up the packet. Deal a card on the left and then a card on the right. Continue alternating as you rapidly deal the packet into two piles on the table. The chosen card will never be face up. As you do the deal, explain, "A lovely mix of face-up and face-down cards." Pick up the pile on the left, turn it over, and place it on top of the pile on the right. Pick up the packet and even it up.

"Now, believe it or not, I have your card face down in this packet of cards." As you fan through the cards, take out each face-down card and place it face down on the table. You appear to be surprised that there are so many face-down cards. Say, "I never said it would be the *only* face-down card." The cards you're removing are, of course, the four jacks and the chosen card. You can tell the selected card because it's the one *immediately following* your key card. Remember the position of the selected card as you place it on the table with the others.

Set the rest of the packet aside. "I'm certain that one of these is your selected card." Pass your hand over the five cards slowly. "This one!" you say, letting your hand drop on top of it. Push the selected card forward from the others. "What was the name of your chosen card?" Ray names it. You turn it over. Right. But the spectators may feel that you've performed a mediocre trick at best.

"As I mentioned, you're a real prince. But you're even better than that." Slowly turn over the four jacks, saying, "You're a prince . . . among princes."

Note

You could use a female volunteer. If so, start with the four queens on top of the deck. Tell your volunteer, "I appreciate this. You're a real lady." At the climax of the trick, say, "As I mentioned, you're a real lady. But you're even better than that." Turn over the queens, saying, "You're a lady . . . among ladies."

Routines for Crazy Cards

I believe that a good routine of card tricks should consist of no more than six tricks or so, ending with a very strong effect. If the group insists, you can always perform more. Three excellent routines can be extracted from this card-trick section. Each routine has variety and considerable spectator involvement.

Open with a trick that appears to be genuine magic, I recommend *A Dizzy Spell* (page 54). Follow up with a humorous trick that has a surprise ending, *Or Not* (page 56). *Say Cheez!* (page 58) is both entertaining and mystifying, plus it has spectator participation. Now a puzzler would be in order, like *Look Ma, No Cards* (page 62). For a colorful climax, do *Happy Marriages* (page 62), which is actually a mini-routine.

If the group wants more, start with *What's in a Name?* (page 66), a baffling spelling trick. *One-Two-Three* (page 68) is that rare trick which becomes more perplexing (and amusing) with each repetition. Time for some real fun with *3–D* (page 70). The climactic trick, *Super Stack* (page 71), generates a great deal of fun.

Here's another routine which can stand on its own, or it can supplement one or both of the others. *The Great Nancini* (page 76) which requires the aid of two spectators, is a snappy opener. The unexpected and funny ending of *Tell Me True* (page 78) makes it perfect for the second trick. There's another surprise for the audience when you do *A Five Spot* (page 80), while *The Hole Card* (page 80) is a bit of blatant skullduggery. In *Can't See It* (page 81), a spectator gets to play with an invisible deck, much to the amusement of all. To top off the routine, *A Real Prince* (page 82) mystifies all and presents your spectator-assistant with a nice compliment.

MAD MONEY

Everyone likes money, so tricks involving it are always of interest. If they're also comical, so much the better.

Which Hand?—1

My inspiration for this trick was observing children play a game in which one child holds a small object in his hand. He places both hands behind his back, and then brings them forward in fists. The other child guesses which hand holds the object.

For your version of the game, any small object will do—a matchbook, the cap of a pen, a nail clipper, a wrapped piece of candy, a large coin, whatever. Invite Nora to play the game with you. The two of you should stand with your sides toward the spectators. Explain, "Nora and I are going to play the 'behind the back' game, using this coin. I'll put my hands behind my back and then bring them forward. Nora must guess which hand holds the coin. Since the rest of you will see where the coin is, I must ask you not to say anything to help Nora."

This warning is important, as you'll see.

Quickly move your hands behind your back, place the coin in one hand or the other, and quickly bring your hands forward in fists. "Which hand?" Before Nora can answer, add, "I make up my mind fast, and you must, too. You have to guess immediately—no stalling."

It doesn't matter whether she guesses correctly or not. Open both hands to show that one is empty, and the other holds the coin. Repeat the procedure. This time, open only the hand she chooses. Do it a third time, opening both hands after she picks.

"We're going to do it differently this time," you say, as you start putting your hands behind your back. "I'll give you some money if you pick the right hand." Put the coin in your left hand and bring your hands forward. If she picks the left hand, open both hands, saying, "You lose. You didn't pick the *right* hand, you picked the *left* hand." If she picks your right hand, say, "You lose. But you would have lost anyway. If you had taken the other hand, I'd have said, 'You didn't pick the *right* hand, you picked the *left* hand.'" Pause briefly to let it sink in. Continue: "This time I'll be as fair as I can be. If you can guess *which hand holds the coin*, I'll give you even more money."

Now you're going to be extremely sneaky. To perform this stunt, you must be wearing a shirt or blouse which is tucked into your trousers or skirt. When you move your hands behind your back this time, tuck the coin under the waistband or belt of the trousers or skirt. The coin should be large enough to stay in position when wedged under the waistband. Instantly bring your hands forward in fists. Nora chooses. Open only the hand she picks, showing that she's wrong.

Again your hands go behind your back. As you present the fists, offer even more money for a correct choice. Offer twice as much money the next time.

Next, as you put your hands behind your back, say, "No money this time." Remove the coin from your waistband and bring your hands forward. This time, open both hands after she chooses.

As you put your hands behind your back, say, "Now I'll offer a great deal of money . . . if you guess the *wrong* hand." Again, tuck the coin under your waistband. Whichever hand Nora chooses, open the *other* hand, showing that it's empty.

Repeat the procedure, offering twice as much money as you did the last time.

Apparently forgetting that you're standing with one hand open and one closed, you say, "Now if you can guess which hand the coin is in, I'll give you twice again the amount I offered last time." Most of the time, your subject will instantly point to your closed hand. But Nora might be somewhat slow. If she is, add "Go ahead. Pick." When she does, show her that the chosen hand is also empty.

A good way to close is to put both hands behind your back, take the coin into one hand, and bring forth both hands wide open. "Now, for no money, pick a hand." Prepare to duck.

Which Hand?—2

Similar to the last trick, this one's almost as silly. You could use this as a follow-up to the last trick. Let's use Ryan this time. Have three small coins in your right pocket. They should all be of the same value. Reach into your pocket and take out two of them. Hand one to Ryan, explaining, "Now we're going to test whether our minds are working together . . . or if they're working at all. Please put your hands behind your back and put the coin in either hand. I'll do the same. Then we'll bring our closed hands forward."

You and Ryan bring your fists forward, he with a coin in one of them, you with a coin in your right hand. Hold your hands directly opposite his. "Okay, show us your coin." If he opens his right hand to show the coin, say, "Ah, your right hand." Open your right hand. "I also chose the right hand." If he opens his left hand to show the coin, open your right hand—the hand directly opposite his left hand—saying, "Ah, a perfect match."

Casually gesture with your open left hand, saying, "Our minds are perfectly attuned." Actually, you're simply demonstrating that your hand is empty. Place the coin (which is in your right hand) into your pocket. As you slide your hand into the pocket, let the coin drop to your cupped fingers. Move the coin so that it's held by the cupped third and fourth fingers. This is called *the finger palm* and is extremely easy. Remove your hand from your pocket and use it naturally, making sure no one gets a glimpse of the coin.

Suddenly you interrupt your routine. "Wait a minute. Maybe we should try it again." Reach into your pocket with your right hand and bring out the third coin, holding it between your thumb and your first two fingers (Illus. 43).

Illus. 43

Another coin is still held by your third and fourth fingers in the finger-palm position. Display the coin and then place your hands behind your back, asking Ryan to do likewise.

You and Ryan bring your fists forward, he with a coin in one of them, you with a coin in each. Follow the same procedure as you did the first time. If, for instance, you matched your right hand with his right hand, you must again match the particular hand; if you matched with hands held opposite one another, you must do this again. Naturally, don't open the other hand.

Again, you both put your hands behind your back. Bring your hands forward and once more you have a match. Repeat this at least once more. By this time, Ryan should have caught on. But if his intelligence doesn't match his eagerness to please, perform an extraordinarily silly trick. You've shown the coin in your left hand, matching his selection. "Now for real magic," you say. Close your left hand, make some mystical motions, and open your right hand. "The coin has magically jumped to the other hand. I'll do it again." Repeat the mystical motions, and show that the coin has returned to your left hand. Perhaps repeat this once more and put the coins away.

Balancing Act

Viewers of this stunt feel that you've either placed some sort of "stickum" on a coin, or that you're an adept juggler. Actually, you're merely skilled at switching fingers, as in *Go Away* (page 43) and *Let's Go to the Hop* (page 44).

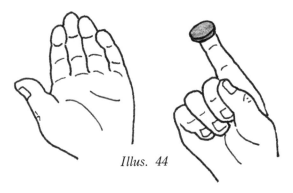

Illus. 44

A large coin works well for this stunt. Balance it on the first finger of your right hand. Your left hand should be slightly cupped and tilted back so that onlookers can't see your palm (Illus. 44).

Apparently the coin resting on your first finger is smacked into your left palm. Immediately your right hand withdraws, and the coin is seen once more, balanced on your first finger. Repeat this rapidly several times.

Actually, as you bring your right hand towards your left, grip the coin between your right first finger and thumb. Simultaneously extend your second right finger and smack your left palm with it. Instantly reverse the actions, and the coin rests once more on the tip of your right first finger. For best effect, perform the action at least three times quite rapidly.

Five or ten minutes of practice should give you a knack for switching fingers.

Thank Q

You'll need 23 coins or poker chips. Toss them on the table.

Kate is always a good sport, so get her to help out. "What's your favorite letter?" you ask. Chances are she *won't* answer Q. "Okay, what's your second favorite letter?" She names another letter other than Q. Ask for her third favorite. Continue through her fifth favorite letter. If she names Q at some point, say, "All right, then we'll use Q." If she gets to her fifth favorite and doesn't name Q, say, "How about Q? Do you like Q?" Chances are that she'll say yes, in which case you'll say, "All right, then, we'll use Q if you insist." If she doesn't like Q, say, "Good. It's best if we use a letter you're not fond of."

With 16 of the coins (or chips), form a circle on the table, and with the remaining seven, form a tail (Illus. 45). Tell Kate to think of a number from ten to twenty. Turn away as you continue: "On the table, I've formed a very peculiar Q. Fortunately, it's also a *magic* Q. Count your number up the tail and around the circle to the left. Then start with the *coin you land on* and count the same number back around the

Illus. 45

circle to the right. But don't go down the tail—just stay on the circle. Be sure to remember which coin you finally land on."

If Kate doesn't know what you want, demonstrate before you turn away. "Suppose you thought of ten. You'd count ten like this." Count up the tail and off to the left. "Then starting with the coin you landed on, you would count ten back around the circle." Show the direction of the count, but don't actually perform it, and then turn away.

When Kate is done, turn back and point to the coin she finally landed on. It's really quite easy. You have seven coins in the tail, so you simply start with the coin to the right of where the tail is connected to the circle; count seven to the right and you have the correct coin.

If you repeat the trick, simply change the number of coins in the tail. But *never* say that's what you're doing.

"We'd better make the circle bigger," you say. Remove two coins from the tail and add them to the circle, spreading out the other coins in the circle.

Now, starting with the coin to the right of where the tail is connected, count *five* to the right to locate the correct coin.

Simple Logic

This exercise in logic can be loads of fun. Place two coins of different values and sizes on the table. Get two volunteers and tell them, "We're going to play a little game. Here are the rules: After I turn my back, each of you will pick up one of the coins and hold it concealed in your hand. Now one of you has to be a liar, and the other has to be a truth-teller. The liar always lies, and the truth-teller always tells the truth. So after I turn away, very quietly decide which of you will lie, and which will tell the truth."

Turn away. When they're ready, turn back. "I'm going to ask a question. Which one should I ask?" After they decide, ask, "Does the liar have the large coin?" If the answer is yes, it means that *the other person* has the larger coin. If the answer is no, it means that the person questioned has the larger coin. Point to each in turn, saying, "You have the small coin, and you have the large coin." Repeat the stunt, this time asking, "Does the liar have the small coin?" Again, a yes answer means that the other person has the coin in question.

"Let's try it again. Only this time, let's see if Tiffany can do it." Have Tiffany give it a try or two; she may succeed. Whether she does or not, tell her, "I'm not sure you understand the system." Then, as fast as you can, recite: "Let me explain how it works: You ask one of the two, 'Does the liar have the large coin?' If you're talking to the liar, he'll say *no* if he has the large coin and *yes* if he has the small coin. If you're talking to the truth-teller, he'll say *yes* if he has the small coin, and *no* if he has the large coin. So if the liar has the large coin, he'll say *no*, and if the truth-teller has the small coin, he'll say *yes*. Clear?"

Probably not.

Whisper to her: "Ask, 'Does the liar have the large coin?' If he answers yes, the other person has it." If necessary, repeat the instructions. Now Tiffany can perform the stunt perfectly. Let her do so. Quite often, someone else may wish to try. If so, repeat your rapid-fire directions, and let her proceed. Call a halt immediately when you see interest wane.

Squeeze Play

For this, you must prepare a special coin, and you must learn a fairly simple sleight. The effort is well worth it, for you'll have a funny trick you can perform on any occasion.

Place a coin in someone's hand. That person squeezes the coin so hard that it bends.

Prepare the coin by placing it halfway in a vise. With a large pliers, bend the coin somewhat. Always carry the coin in your right-hand pocket, and you can perform anytime. In that same pocket, you should have a handkerchief.

Start by putting your hands in your pockets. Grip the bent coin in your curled right third and fourth fingers. Remove your hand from the pockets as you ask someone to lend you a coin of the same value as your prepared coin. Take the proffered coin with your right hand, gripping it between your thumb and your first and second fingers. Don't be afraid that anyone can see the bent coin.

Toss the borrowed coin into your left hand. Pick out a spectator who's known for his frugality. Clyde, for instance, is quite thrifty. Ask him to hold out his hand. "Now when I put the coin in your hand, hold it really tight." With your left hand, place the coin in his hand. He's not doing it right, however. Have him open his hand. Take the coin with your right hand, gripping it between your thumb and your first two fingers, as before. Now you'll perform a sleight known as *The Bobo Switch*. Presumably you once more toss the coin into your left hand; actually, you retain the borrowed coin and toss the bent coin into your left hand, where you hold it in a loose fist (Illus. 46). Your right hand, of course, holds the borrowed coin. Immediately make a tight fist with your right hand and shake your fist up and down, as though with the

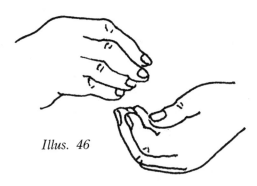

Illus. 46

intensity of your squeezing. "You have to really squeeze it. Let's try again."

With your left hand, place the bent coin into his hand. By guiding with your left fingers, make sure he closes his fingers on it immediately. Meanwhile, you've let your right hand drop to your side, fingers loosely cupping the borrowed coin.

Reach into your right-hand pocket. Leave the coin there as you remove the handkerchief. Shake the handkerchief open, as you say, "Squeeze really hard, because I'm going to try to make the coin disappear." Cover his hand with the handkerchief. Make mystic waves over it. "Hocus-pocus! The coin's now gone." Whip the handkerchief away. "Please open your hand."

He does so. "Good heavens, look at that! You squeezed it so hard you bent it out of shape. Sorry, I can only make *normal* coins vanish."

Let everyone get a good look at the bent coin and then put it away.

That's How Your Money Goes

This swindle will make people think you're a superb sleight-of-hand artist.

Borrow a handkerchief and a large coin. "Ladies and gentlemen, you're about to see an amazing demonstration of prestidigitation. Watch carefully!"

As you proceed, make your gestures as grand as possible. Display the coin in your left hand between your thumb and fingertips. With your right hand, place the handkerchief over it. Take the coin and the handkerchief in your right hand. (Illus. 47). Show that your left hand is empty. Have three or

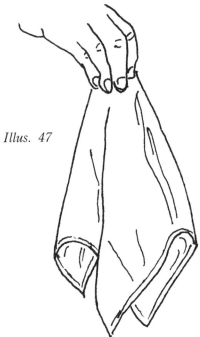

Illus. 47

four spectators reach under the handkerchief to verify that the coin is still there. Say to each, "Is the coin there? Good."

Apparently you place the coin and handkerchief on the palm of your left hand. Suddenly you smack your right hand down on the handkerchief. Pull the handkerchief away; the coin is gone! Show both sides of the handkerchief and return it to the owner.

What happened to the coin? The last person who checked under the handkerchief—Lionel—is your confederate. He took the coin and casually dropped his hand to his side. When all attention was on you, he stuck his hand in his pocket and left the coin there.

You could repay the person who loaned you the coin and call it quits, letting everyone think that you're a master magician. The following closing is more fun, however:

"The magic has worked, ladies and gentlemen, and the coin has disappeared forever. An evil spirit has taken the coin to a mysterious hideaway, depriving this poor man of his hard-earned money. Yes, some corrupt demon has stolen the lawful property of this poor, desperate . . ."

Lionel, your confederate, stands up. "All right, all right! I'll give it back." He returns the coin to the lender.

Routine for Mad Money

Start by saying something like, "Everyone likes money, mainly to spend. But, there are so many other interesting things you can do with it. For instance . . ."

Which Hand?-1 and *Which Hand?-2* (pages 86 and 88) should open your act well. *Balancing Act* (page 90), then, is a nice change of pace. Spectators also participate with the tricks *Thank Q* (page 91) and *Simple Logic* (page 93).

If you decide to do the necessary preparation, now would be a good time to perform the extremely funny *Squeeze Play* (page 94). Closing with *That's How Your Money Goes* (page 96) is quite effective.

MONKEYSHINES

In this section you'll find tricks with dice, a handkerchief, a cracker, rope, crayons, balloons, candy, safety pins, and a variety of other materials. Some of these tricks require preparation.

Roll Them Bones

You'll need at least four dice, but use six to make the trick more interesting. Toss the six dice out on the table.

"Would someone please pick up a number of dice." Let's say George picks up four dice. Push the others to one side. "In a moment I'd like you to roll those dice out on the table. Suppose that when they stop rolling, I immediately announce the total of the top sides. That would demonstrate that I am a mathematical whiz. Instead, I'm going to perform magic. I'll announce the *combined total* of the top and bottom sides. Go ahead; roll them."

George rolls out the four dice. When they come to rest, you *instantly* announce, "Twenty-eight."

Together you add up the top sides of the dice. Turn over the dice and add up the bottom side. Together the total is twenty-eight. You're a marvel.

Suppose Esther takes six dice for the next try. When the dice stop rolling, you immediately announce, "Forty-two." Again, you're correct.

You can perform this feat several times, but each time the number of dice must be different, because you want to come up with a different total each time. The secret is that the two sides of any die add up to seven. So to come up with the right total, all you have to do is multiply by seven the number of dice thrown.

This routine can be particularly funny if you pretend to be under great strain. "No one understands the stress, the tension of trying to perform real magic," you might gasp. Or you say, "Oh, the intense concentration is giving me a headache!"

If someone does figure out the secret and discloses it to the group, you might, in mock petulance, say, "Well, I'm still a mathematical whiz. Do you think it's easy multiplying by seven?"

Loaded Die

Rev. Raymond Amiro came up with this idea. In this version of the trick, you'll use a die which you claim is loaded. Most often you produce the die yourself and toss it onto the table. You can also pick up a die which has been used in a game and say, "My goodness, I believe that this is one of those loaded dice I've heard about."

You then set the die on the table with the 1 side up and the 5 side facing you. "All you have to do is tap it on top and you can get the number you want." Tap the 1 side twice. "I want a 2, for instance." Pick up the die, holding it between your

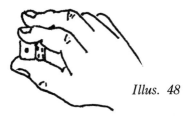

Illus. 48

first finger and thumb (Illus. 48). The 1 side faces the spectators and the 5 side is against your thumb. Revolve your hand clockwise to show the other side. But as you do, move your first finger back and move your thumb forward, turning the die clockwise so that it moves to the next clockwise number. The larger move of your hand completely disguises the lesser move. Now you're displaying a 2 (Illus. 49). Reverse the moves, showing the 1 again.

Illus. 49

Set the die on the table, rotating it slightly so that the 4 now faces you. Say, "Now we need a 3. Tap the die three times. Pick up the die so that the 1 shows, and the 4 side is against your thumb. Perform the same moves, showing the 1, then the 3, and back to the 1.

Again, return the die to the table, rotating it once more so that a 2 now faces you. Tap the die once, saying, "Just a question of tapping on top." Pause a moment. "Let's see, now we need a 4. Tap the die four times. This time when you display the other side, a 5 will show. "Whoops! I must have tapped it one too many times." Show the 1 and return the die to the table, revolving it so that the 3 now faces you.

"Let's *really* get the 4." Carefully tap the die four times. Display the die again, showing a 4 on the opposite side.

Next time you go for 6. Tap the die six times. Pick it up and when you turn it over to show the other side, do *not* perform the sleight. A 6 is the actual opposite side. Show the 1 again and return the die to the table.

"Hmmm, we've tried everything but the one." Tap the die once. Pick it up and turn it over, using the rotating sleight. The 1 doesn't appear. "I wonder what happened." Very deliberately turn the die with your *left hand*, revealing that the bottom is side 1. "Oh! It only came halfway."

Dippy Die

To perform this trick, you'll have to memorize a bit and practise a little, but no particular skill is required, and the entertainment value is enormous.

A little preparation is required. Prepare a 3″ × 5″ (7.5 × 13 cm) file card in advance, or use a business card.

In either case, you must take a pen—a marking pen is best—and make little circles on the card, so that the card somewhat resembles a domino. Be sure to color in the circles so that they can be easily seen. On one side, draw two circles, as shown in Illus. 50.

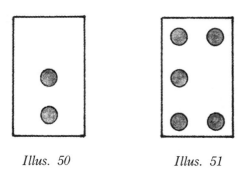

Illus. 50   *Illus. 51*

Turn over the card, as though you were turning the page of a book. On this other side, draw five circles, as shown in Illus 51.

Let's assume that you're sitting around with friends. If you're going to use a business card, casually mark the card while chatting, letting the card rest on your tilted left hand (assuming you're right-handed), shielding what you're doing. In a restaurant, as you mark the card, you can rest it on your raised menu. Incidentally, the printing on one side of the business card shouldn't be a problem; just make sure that you mark that printed side with the two dots.

The key to this stunt is the way you hold and turn the card. For clarity, the illustrations will show the use of a file card.

"Did you ever play card craps?" you ask, keeping your card out of sight. Your friends are likely to answer no.

"Me neither. Until the other night. I met a stranger in a restaurant, and he asked me that very question. 'Did you ever play card craps?' I said, 'No.' He said, 'Nothing to it. I have a magic card that's just like a die. It's a perfectly flat card. On one side is a 1, on the other is a 2, on the other is a 3, on the other is a 4, on the other is a 5, and on the other is a 6.' I said, 'That's impossible.' He said, 'No, that's magic. Here's the way the game goes: We look at both sides of the card. If the two sides total 7, you lose the bet. Then I do it again, doubling the bet. And if I get a 7 this time, you lose . . . *providing* I get a 7 with two numbers different from the first ones. If I don't, I lose.' I said, 'You've got a bet,' and I put down some money."

Take out the card and hold it in your left hand, so that the number, from the spectator's view, seems to be 6. See Illus. 52. *All the remaining illustrations for this trick will be from the spectators' point of view.* Say, "6 on one side." Bring up your

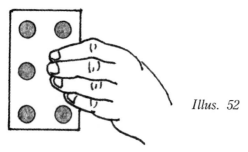

Illus. 52

right hand, fingers behind covering the bottom dot and thumb in front (Illus. 53). Quickly rotate your right hand counterclockwise, letting go with your left hand. You're now apparently displaying a 1. Say, "And 1 on this side. 6 and 1 are seven. I gave the man the money."

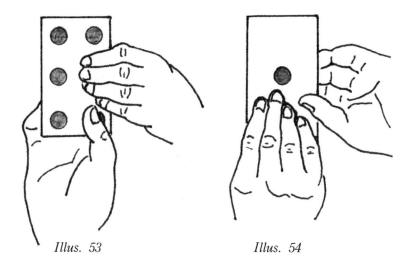

Illus. 53 *Illus. 54*

"I said, 'Now we'll double the bet. Let's see you get a 7 with two numbers different from the first ones.' And he did it."

Grip the card with your left hand, thumb on the front and fingers on the back (Illus. 54). Your fingers should cover the spot on the left side. Rapidly rotate your left hand so that the back of your hand is towards the spectators, and the card is turned end for end. As you do so, let go with your right hand. The spectators are now looking at 4 dots (Illus. 55). Say, "4 on one side."

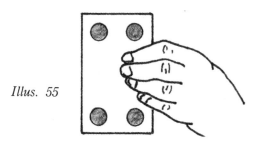

Illus. 55

As before, grip the bottom of the card with your right fingers on the back of the card and right thumb in front. Turn the card so that the back of your fingers are to the front. You're apparently displaying 3 dots. Say, "And 3 on this side. 4 and 3 are seven. I gave the man the money."

Without changing your grip, drop your hand to your side as you say, "I told the fellow, 'That's fine, but how about giving me a turn with the card?' He said, 'Okay, I'll give you two tries. Each time double or nothing. So I grabbed that card and went to work."

When you display the numbers for your turn, the handling will be different. Grasp the card in the usual manner with your left hand, as shown in Illus. 54 (page 103). Turn the card end-for-end, displaying an apparent 6 spots. Say, "6 on this side."

Now for the different handling. Turn your left hand so that the card's long side is parallel to the floor. With your right hand, grip the card on the right side, fingers on the back of the card and right thumb in front (Illus. 56). Turn over the

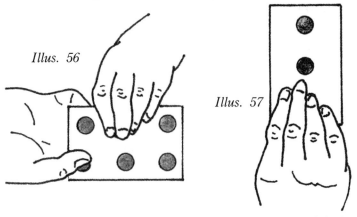

Illus. 56

Illus. 57

card with your right hand. Immediately turn your right hand palm-up so that you display the spots as shown in Illus. 57. Say, "And 3 on this side. 6 and 3 are nine. I lost again, but I bet one more time."

Revolve your right hand, turning it palm-down. Take the left-hand grip in the usual manner (Illus. 58). Turn the card end-for-end, displaying 4 spots. Say, "4 spots on this side."

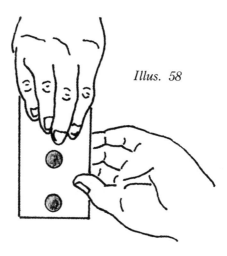

Illus. 58

As before, turn your left hand so that the card's long side is nearly parallel to the floor. Your right hand grips the card on the right side, fingers on the back of the card covering the dot and your right thumb in front. Turn over the card so that you display 1 dot. Say, "Whoops! One dot on this side. 4 and 1 are five. I lost again."

At this point, if you wish, you can tear the card into little pieces, saying, "I was so disgusted I tore up the card and called it quits." Some spectators may be baffled as to how you accomplished this magical feat. With children, I almost always close by tearing up the card.

Here's the way I prefer to finish:

Drop your hand to your side, saying, "The stranger said, 'Let's have another game. It's my turn with the magic card.' I said, 'Sure. Double or nothing. Only this time, no tricky turns. Just drop the card on the table . . . and then turn it over on the table.' He said, 'Okay,' and took the card."

Drop the card on the table. "5 dots on this side." Flip the card over. "And 2 dots on this side. 5 and 2 are seven."

Rip the card to shreds. "The moral is, 'Never gamble with strangers.'"

Notes

If you use a business card rather than a file card, you can adequately hide the dots with one or two fingers, rather than three.

The moves aren't really difficult. Mark a card and follow the directions. In short order, the moves will be second nature to you.

Poof Paff Piff!

The point of this trick is to connect two safety pins and try to separate them by pulling them apart. Naturally it doesn't work—*until* you say the proper magic words.

First of all, large safety pins aren't as easy to find as they once were. Even when you *do* find them in the baby section of your local store, they usually have plastic heads. The plastic head locks the pointed bar in place, preventing you from performing the trick. You need *all-metal* safety pins. In the *sewing section* of that same store you'll likely find all-metal, two-inch pins; they're perfect for this trick.

Next, learn exactly how to separate the pins. Open Pin A and, in your right hand, hold it at the small end, with the pointed bar on the right (Illus. 59). In your left hand, hold Pin

Pin A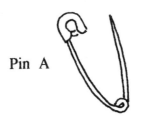

Illus. 59

B at the small end, so that the pointed bar is on top (Illus. 60). Note that Pin B is shaded for clarity. Insert the head of Pin A between the bars of Pin B (Illus. 61). Close Pin A and then turn it over counterclockwise (Illus. 62). Hold Pin A at

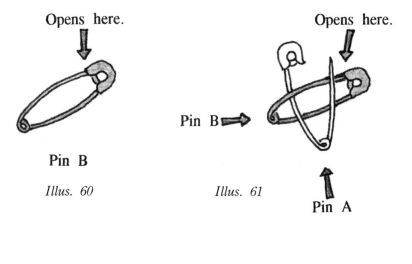

Illus. 60

Illus. 61

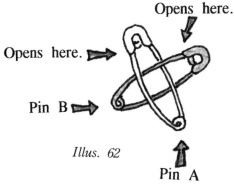

Illus. 62

the small end in your right hand, and Pin B at the small end in your left hand. *The ends must be held firmly.* Snap the pins apart, rapidly sliding Pin A to the right and slightly towards you. The solid bar of Pin A pulls down the pointed bar of Pin

B, allowing Pin A to escape. The pointed bar of Pin B snaps back into place. Needless to say, the entire action happens too fast for the eye to follow. The positioning of the pins must be *exactly* as described.

Now for the trick itself. Show the pins and connect them as described above. "Although these pins are connected," you say, "all I need to do is say the magic words and they'll separate." Take the pins at the small ends. "Poof paff piff!" Pull Pin A straight down. The pins, of course, won't separate.

"Maybe I didn't say the words right. Let me try again. Paff poof piff!" Again they fail to separate. You try again with the words "Poof piff paff!" No good. You're very discouraged. "I'm sure those are the right words. Can anyone help me?" Someone is bound to suggest you try "Piff paff poof!" Hold the pins in readiness, saying, "I'm sure that's right. Would you mind saying that again?" When the person does so, separate the pins. Hold up one pin in each hand. "Bless you. I couldn't have done it without you."

Stick Pin

Use a good pair of scissors to cut off the colored tip from a matchstick. Now stick a safety pin right through the middle of the matchstick. Move the matchstick to the middle of the pin (Illus. 63). Now you're ready to perform a semi-miracle.

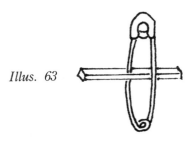

Illus. 63

"This fabulous device has the power to tell you whether a wish will come true. If the matchstick passes through the metal of the pin, your wish will come true. If it doesn't, the wish will *never* come true. For this to work, the wish *must* be stated aloud. For instance, I wish to become a millionaire. Watch."

Hold the pin in your left hand and place the first finger of your right hand behind the matchstick (Illus. 64). Pull the

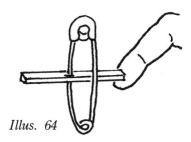

Illus. 64

matchstick towards you as though trying to pull it through the pin. As the wood hits the metal, let your finger slide off the matchstick with a snap. Apparently the matchstick passes right through the metal. You may succeed on your first try. If not, keep trying; you should get the hang of it after several attempts.

What actually happens, of course, is that your snapping motion causes the matchstick to bounce off the metal and describe a semicircle. The other end of the matchstick now rests against the pin on the near right side. The illusion is perfect: Evidently the matchstick passed right through the metal. Even after practice, it may take you a few tries to get the matchstick to end up right next to the metal on the near side. Don't make excuses; simply make a different wish and try again.

After having one or two of your wishes verified, say, "I believe someone else should give this gadget a try." Choose

Sheila. Have her state her wish and then guide her through the proper procedure with the gadget. If she fails at first, have her try again with a different wish. When she finally succeeds, share her glee and congratulate her on her forthcoming good fortune.

As long as interest persists, work with other spectators in the same way. Chances are, many will get the hang of it. Even so, they still may not guess the secret of the gadget.

It's Crackers!

To perform this amusing stunt, all you need is a small round cracker and a little practice.

Announce that you're about to execute an astonishing miracle. Call attention to the cracker, which you hold in the palm of your right hand. Exert slight pressure so that the cracker can be retained in your palm. Bring your right hand in front of your left, a bit below your left fingers. Fold up the fingers of your left hand with the left edge of your right hand, retaining the cracker in your right hand. Illus. 65 shows the

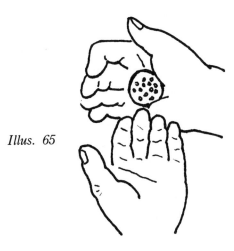

Illus. 65

position as you begin the rearward movement of your right hand. The illusion is that you've dropped the cracker into your left hand.

"To make this work," you say, "we'll need some magic stardust." Reach into your pocket with your right hand. Bring out your hand in a loose fist, concealing the cracker.

"Now we'll just sprinkle the hand with the magic stardust and see what happens."

Hold your right hand about 8″ (20 cm) above your left hand and crumble the cracker, letting the powdery crumbs fall on your left hand. Open your left hand, showing that the cracker has disappeared.

For a moment or two, most will think that you've performed a fantastic trick. Then it will dawn on everyone where that magic stardust came from.

Rolling Along

This stunt can be performed with a small, round crayon, a pencil, a pen with its cap removed, or even a piece of notepad-size paper rolled into a tight cylinder.

Let's assume you're using a pen with its cap removed. Set the pen on a table about 8″ (20 cm) from the near edge and parallel to that edge. "Let's see if it will follow my finger," you say. Leaning forward, reach over the pen and place your finger down. Move your finger slowly away from the pen. Nothing happens. Try a few more times.

"Maybe I can push it." Place your finger 6″ (15 cm) or so on the near side of the pen. Move your finger forward a few inches. After a few failures, the pen rolls slowly away from you.

Onlookers are truly amazed since, evidently, some mysterious power has caused the pen to move. That mysterious power is your breath. With your lips slightly parted, softly exhale just behind the pen. *Exhale* is the proper word; if you *blow*, your lips might move too much.

A good closing is to say, "Now that I'm successful at moving pens, I'm going to try moving larger objects. Come here a minute, will you, Mark?" He'll probably step closer. "Gosh, it's working already!"

Use a perfectly round pencil for the experiment, since most pencils have square edges, making it hard to roll them.

Love Knot

Any stunt can be enhanced if you have a little story to go with it. Here's a good example.

A moment's preparation is necessary. Tie a small square knot in the corner of a handkerchief. Place the cloth in your pocket or purse, so that the knot can be readily grasped and concealed when you remove the handkerchief.

Let's assume that Margaret is doing the stunt. Take out the handkerchief with your right hand and hold the cloth so that the knot is hidden by your fingers and the rest of the handkerchief hangs down.

"I want to find out if my husband *really* loves me. Obviously, the best bet is to use this handkerchief."

With your left hand, pick up the bottom corner of the handkerchief and place the corner so that it's loosely held in your right hand next to the knotted end of the cloth.

Snap your right arm downward as you would when trying to snap a whip. As you snap, release the corner you just placed in your hand. At the same time, say, "He loves me."

Place the bottom corner of the handkerchief in your hand again. Repeat the snapping action, saying, "He loves me not."

Do it again, saying, "He loves me."

Once more snap the handkerchief, only this time, release the knotted corner and hang on to the other corner. As you snap, say, "He loves me not."

Raise your hand so that all can see the knot. "Hey, look, I made a knot. A love knot." Pause. "But is it a 'loves me' knot, or a 'loves me not' knot?"

A Good Cut

Needed: a sheet of 8½″ × 11″ (22 × 28 cm) typing paper and a pair of scissors.

"With amazing skill, I'm going to show you an example of paper-cutting."

Fold the sheet of paper, following the steps shown in Illus. 66. In each drawing, the fold is indicated by the dotted line.

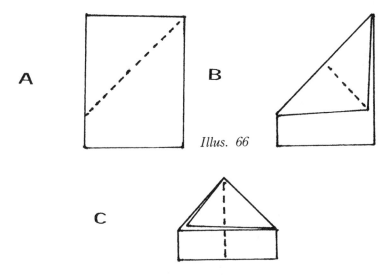

Illus. 66

In *A*, grasp the upper left corner of the paper and fold it towards you, downwards and diagonally. In *B*, grasp the corner on the upper right side and fold it towards you, also downwards and diagonally. In *C*, grasp the right side of the packet and move it towards you, folding the packet in half

Turn to Kristen, saying, "I said 'with amazing skill.' The fact is, I have no skill at cutting paper. It's up to you to provide the skill. I'll provide the instructions."

Hand her the scissors. There's a dotted line shown in Illus. 67 that indicates where you run your finger to show Kristen

Illus. 67

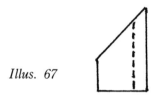

where she'll cut. Make the cut about one inch (2.5 cm) from the right side. "Do you think you can cut across here?"

Hold the paper so she can make her cut. Hold the one-inch (2.5-cm) strip in one hand. With your other hand, shake the larger section, and look disappointed when pieces fall to the floor. "Kristen, I asked you to cut across, and now we get pieces."

Unfold the smaller section and display the cross. "Oh, I guess you were able to cut a cross after all."

The Magic Balloon

Blow up a balloon and stick a small piece of clear cellophane tape on it. Make sure you place the tape in a spot you'll find easily.

Display the balloon. Stick a pin or needle right into it. The balloon won't burst because you made sure to stick the pin through the cellophane tape. Pull out the pin and proudly hold up the balloon once more.

The balloon will very gradually deflate. So you'd better cover your tracks. Connie will be happy to help out. Say to her, "Connie, as you notice, I have a magic balloon." Hand her the pin. "Just stick this balloon with the pin." Naturally, the balloon bursts.

Eye the remains ruefully. "Well, it used to be a magic balloon."

Ring Around the Collar

Everyone but your volunteer assistant knows how you perform this feat of magic. Some preparation is necessary.

Get a section of newspaper. Tear off a 2″ (5 cm) strip the full length of the paper that's about 22 inches (55 cm) long. Tear off seven more strips. Take two of the strips and glue one to the other at their ends. You now have a strip about 43 inches (98 cm) long. Glue the ends together so that the strip becomes a hoop or ring.

Make two more hoops just like the first one. The next strip must be made into a hoop which interlocks with one of the others. You'll end up with two separate hoops and two which are interlocked (Illus. 68).

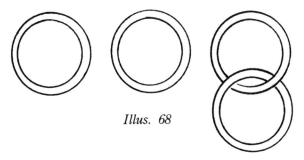

Illus. 68

Place all the rings into your purse or paper bag, and you'll be ready to perform.

First, get a good-natured volunteer. Tim's a good choice.

Remove a paper ring from the bag, saying, "I'm going to attempt a difficult feat of magic with this ring." Have Tim stand facing the spectators. Slip the paper ring over his left arm so that it's about at biceps level. Tell Tim, "Please place your hand on your hip so that there's no way I can get the ring off." He does so. "Now this amazing feat can't be performed unless you close your eyes and don't open them until I tell you to. Okay?" He agrees. "Now close your eyes."

As soon as Tim shuts his eyes, take the linked rings from your purse or bag and place one of the rings over Tim's head so that the ring encircles his neck. The other ring hangs behind his neck. As you do this, chat about how important it is that he keep his eyes shut.

Make sure you speak loudly and incessantly. Slowly tear the other ring, so that you can take it from his arm. Wad up the paper ring you just removed and stick it into your pocket.

"Hocus-pocus! Now open your eyes." He does so. "Notice that the ring on your arm has now mysteriously jumped from your arm to around your neck." Give him only a second or two to absorb this, because you don't want him toying with the ring around his neck. "Now let's attempt something even more difficult."

Take the last paper ring from your purse or bag and slip it onto Tim's left arm as before. Again, have him place his hand on his hip to keep the ring from escaping. *Have him place his right hand on top of his head.* "This eliminates any possibility of trickery," you explain.

Have him close his eyes. As you babble on about the importance of keeping his eyes shut, turn around the ring on his neck so that the ring at his back now hangs in front. As before, tear and remove the ring from his arm. Wad up the ring and stick it in your pocket.

"Hocus-pocus! Open your eyes." He does so. "Not only has the ring escaped from your arm, but it's now linked with the other ring around your neck." Gesture towards Tim.

"You've done a great job." Lead the applause and take a deep bow.

Note

You can make this a trick for the entire group by asking all present to close their eyes along with your assistant. The request, as well as the group's response, should evoke considerable hilarity, and many will think you're a fabulous magician.

Over Your Head

I first saw this performed by Slydini. You need a volunteer who's a good sport. Holly would be the perfect choice. Have her sit in a chair while you stand, facing her. Both of you are sideways to onlookers.

"I'd like to try an experiment in which we test your reflexes," you explain. Tear off about a quarter of a page of a newspaper and wad it up tightly. Do this with two more quarter-pages. Set two of the wads aside and hold one in your right hand.

"Hold out your right hand, palm up. I'll touch this paper wad to your hand three times. At the count of three, I want you to close your hand and hang on to it. Ready?"

Raise your right hand above Holly's head and bring down your hand so that it touches her hand. As you touch the hand, say, "One." Make the same movement, saying, "Two." The third time, release the wad of paper so that she can grab it as you say, "Three."

"Do you have the paper wad?" When she shows that she does, tell her, "Your reflexes are excellent." Take the paper wad, saying, "Let's try it again." Go through the same procedure, again letting her grab the paper wad on the count of three.

"Do you have the paper wad?" When she shows it, say, "You're the best I've ever seen. Once more."

Take the paper wad from Holly and do the first two counts as before. But as you bring your hand up the third time, toss the paper wad over Holly's head. In precisely the same manner as before, bring down your hand and touch it to Holly's hand, which she closes as you move your hand away.

"Do you have the paper wad?" She doesn't. "I wonder what happened." Onlookers know and are much amused, but Holly doesn't know.

Take another of the paper wads and repeat the mysterious disappearance. You might pretend to be suspicious that Holly is up to no good. Ask her, "What did you do with that?"

Take the last paper wad and perform the stunt once more. The spectators will be more amused at each repetition. If Holly hasn't caught on, feign puzzlement, saying, "Well, your reflexes are excellent, so it's probably not your fault. Anyway, thanks for the help."

If Holly does catch on earlier, admit that she caught you and congratulate her on her astuteness.

All Tied Up

For this snappy trick, the brainchild of Karrell Fox, you'll need a piece of rope 4' or 5' (1.2 or 1.5 m) long. Get two volunteers to stand on either side of you. Hold your hands wrist to wrist. Have the volunteers loop the rope around your wrists. (Illus. 69). They then pull the rope quite tight. The rope must now be crossed as shown in Illus. 70. Have the appropriate volunteer swing his rope around front, while the other volunteer retains pressure. Then the other volunteer drops his end on the inside, while his partner retains pressure.

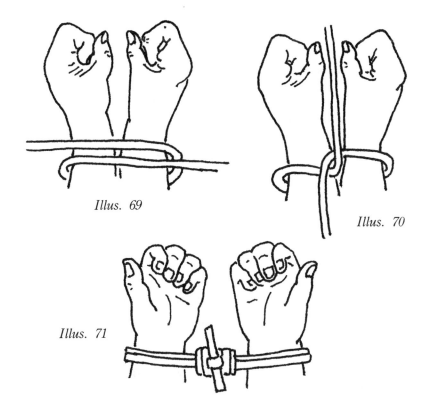

Illus. 69

Illus. 70

Illus. 71

Make sure you press your wrists together *firmly* during this next stage. One volunteer holds his end of the rope firmly while the other winds his end of rope between your hands a few times. The other end is wound around in the opposite direction. Encourage them both to exert pressure, but don't let them get the rope *between* your wrists. The rope *must* be wrapped around outside.

After this, the ends are crossed on top and firmly wrapped *around* your wrists several times. The volunteers tie the rope on top, making as many knots as they wish.

It would appear that your wrists are securely bound. Actually, to free your hands, you need only turn your right hand clockwise and your left hand counterclockwise (Illus. 71).

Ask one of the volunteers to cover your hands with a jacket or a sweater. Immediately say to the two, "You have to be standing in exactly the right spot for this to work." Release your right hand, and from behind, move the volunteer on your right around a bit, saying "Just move forward a little bit, please." Instantly, return your hand under the jacket and struggle as you apparently try to release yourself. If you're sneaky enough, neither volunteer will be fully aware of what you've done.

Do the same service for the volunteer on your left, again returning your hand beneath the jacket to continue struggling to release yourself. Obviously, other spectators will be amused at your little game.

Continue the byplay until your assistants catch on. Then, holding the rope at the fingertips of one hand, let the jacket drop to the floor. Hold up the rope and take a bow.

It's in the Bag

The original idea for this trick is by Don Tanner.

All you need to perform this extraordinary trick is a medium-size (or large) paper bag. Experiment to find which size bag works best for you. About 1″ (2.5 cm) from the bottom of one of the long sides of the bag, cut out a square

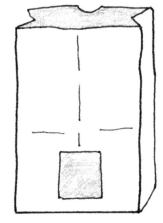

Illus. 72

about 4″ × 4″ (10 × 10 cm) (Illus. 72). From another bag, cut a square piece about 5″ × 5″ (13 × 13 cm). Place this piece inside the bag so that it overlaps the hole on all sides. Secure the piece *at the top* with strips of cellophane tape. Now you have a convenient flap inside the bag.

With a heavy marker, print on the opposite side of the bag the word MAGIC. You should have a ring on your left hand, a watch on your left wrist, and a folded handkerchief in your left pocket.

To perform, hold up the bag so that all can see. The flap, of course, is in the side *away* from the audience.

"Here, ladies and gentlemen, we have a magic bag." Point to the word MAGIC printed on the bag. "This is how you can tell."

With the flap side down, turn the bag so that the audience can see inside. "As you can see, the bag is as empty as a magician's promises." Clearly, the bag is empty. To emphasize this, hold the bag loosely at the sides, turn it upside down, and shake it. Of course, the flap side is away from the audience.

Now turn over the bag so that the bottom rests on your left hand. You may have to dig your left thumb into the hole to hold the bag in place.

Wave your hand over the bag, say a few magic words, and reach inside. Lift up the flap, remove the ring from your left hand, and produce the ring. Hold it up so that all can see it. "A ring from the magic bag." Set the ring aside.

Again wave and say the magic words. Reach inside, lift the flap, remove your wristwatch, and produce it. If your watch has a flexible band, you'll have to release your grip on the bag with your left hand. Simply press the side of the bag against your body with your right forearm. Don't worry about any trouble you may have getting the watch off your wrist. As you struggle, comment. "The magic bag just doesn't want to let go." When you produce the watch, say, "No wonder it didn't want to let go. A valuable watch!" Set it aside.

Cough lightly a few times. Hold the bag at the top in your right hand as you casually reach into your pocket with your left hand and remove the folded handkerchief. Cough again and pat your lips with the folded handkerchief. Still holding the folded handkerchief, set the bag on top of your left hand once more. Wave mystically and say the magic words. Reach into the bag, lift the flap, and grasp the handkerchief by one corner. Shake it inside the bag briefly to open the cloth as much as possible, then produce it, waving it wildly so that it opens fully. "A handkerchief! Yet another miracle!"By this time, some (at least) spectators will have a good idea of what you're up to. Nevertheless, even they'll be momentarily startled by your next production.

"One final dip into the magic bag!" Push your left hand right through the flap. As your right hand enters the bag, your right wrist and forearm will have to push the bag downwards so that the bag rides several inches over your left forearm. Simultaneously, with your right hand, grip your left wrist or the bottom portion of your left hand and "lift" your

Illus. 73   **MAGIC**

hand out of the top of the bag (Illus. 73). All of this should be done quite rapidly. "A human hand!" you declare.

At first, the sight of the left hand emerging from the top of the bag has a shocking effect, usually followed by laughter. Hold your hand in sight only briefly. Then turn your back to the audience and pull the bag off your arm. Toss the bag aside, or quickly fold it and stuff it into your pocket. Turn back and take a bow, saying, "No applause, please; I already got a nice hand."

Routines for Monkeyshines

Nine of the tricks in this section can be combined to form an impromptu routine. If you have several dice in your pocket, or if dice are available, perform the first two tricks: *Roll Them Bones* (page 98) and *Loaded Die* (page 99). Then lead naturally into the tale of the *Dippy Die* (page 101). You can make the "dippy die" as you address the group, or have the card prepared in advance.

I often carry two loose safety pins in my pocket so that I can perform *Poof Paff Piff* ! (page 106) at a moment's notice. I also carry a matchstick pierced by a safety pin for *Stick Pin* (page 108).

If it's convenient to borrow a round cracker, you can perform the hilarious *It's Crackers!* (page 110). In *Rolling Along* (page 111), you display your telekinetic ability by mysteriously causing a crayon or pen to roll.

The only preparation needed for the next trick, *Love Knot* (page 112), is to secretly tie a knot in one end of a handkerchief.

A Good Cut (page 113), which involves the aid of a spectator, is a puzzling and comical trick, making it perfect for your finale. All that's needed is a sheet of paper and a pair of scissors.

The remaining six tricks in this section call for a situation in which you're *performing*. You don't need to be on a stage or platform, but it's best if the entire group is seated in front of you, and you're putting on a show. Some of the tricks *could* be performed in a semiformal situation, notably *Over Your Head* (page 117), and *The Magic Balloon* (page 114). Considerable preparation is necessary for most of these, so you may want to eliminate some of these tricks from your routine.

The order in which you do the tricks isn't particularly important. You should start with a trick to get everyone's attention and end with what you consider the best. *The Magic Balloon* (page 114) should get things going with a real bang.

Close with *It's in the Bag* (page 120), a very strong trick.

In between, you can do any or all of these: *Ring Around the Collar* (page 115), *Over Your Head* (page 117), and *All Tied Up* (page 118). The last, in particular, always gets a solid audience response.

MASTERY LEVELS CHART & INDEX

TRICK	PAGE	EASY	HARDER	ADVANCED
			DIFFICULTY	
All Tied Up	118		*	
And Slide Again	15			*
Balancing Act	90		*	
Blind Dates	35	*		
Bouncy Band	25		*	
Candy Is Dandy	22			*
Can't See It	81	*		
Dippy Die	101			*
Disjointed Digit	40		*	
Dizzy Spell	54			*
Ergo	32	*		
Eye of the Needle	21		*	
Five Spot	80	*		
Give 'Em the Slip	31	*		
Go Away	43	*		
Good Cut	113		*	
Gotcha!	37		*	
Great Nancini	76	*		
Happy Marriages	62			*
Hole Card	80		*	
How Oh-Old Are You?	36		*	
Incredible Knot	16			*
Incredible Shrinking Finger	42		*	
It's Crackers!	110	*		
It's in the Bag	120		*	

Knot at All	18				*
Let's Go to the Hop!	44	*			
Loaded Die	99				*
Look Ma, No Cards	62	*			
Love Knot	112		*		
Magic Balloon	114	*			
Mind Under Matter	34	*			
No Noose Is Good Noose	12		*		
One-Two-Three	68		*		
Or Knot to Be	19		*		
Or Not	56		*		
Over Your Head	117		*		
Poof Paff Piff!	106		*		
Real Prince	82		*		
Revolving Wrist	45		*		
Ring Around the Collar	115		*		
Roll Them Bones	98	*			
Rolling Along	111		*		
Say Cheez!	58				*
Simple Logic	93		*		
Sliding Knot	13		*		
Squeeze Play	94				*
Stick Pin	108		*		
Sticky Knife—1	47	*			
Sticky Knife—2	49		*		
String Out—1	9		*		
String Out—2	11				*
Super Stack	71		*		

Tell Me True	78	*		
Telling Time	30	*		
Thank Q	91	*		
That Band Really Jumps	26		*	
That's How Your Money Goes	96	*		
3-D	70		*	
What's in a Name?	66		*	
Which Hand—1	86		*	
Which Hand—2	88		*	
You Can Count on Your Body	35		*